YVES SAINT LAURENT

THE PERFECTION OF STYLE

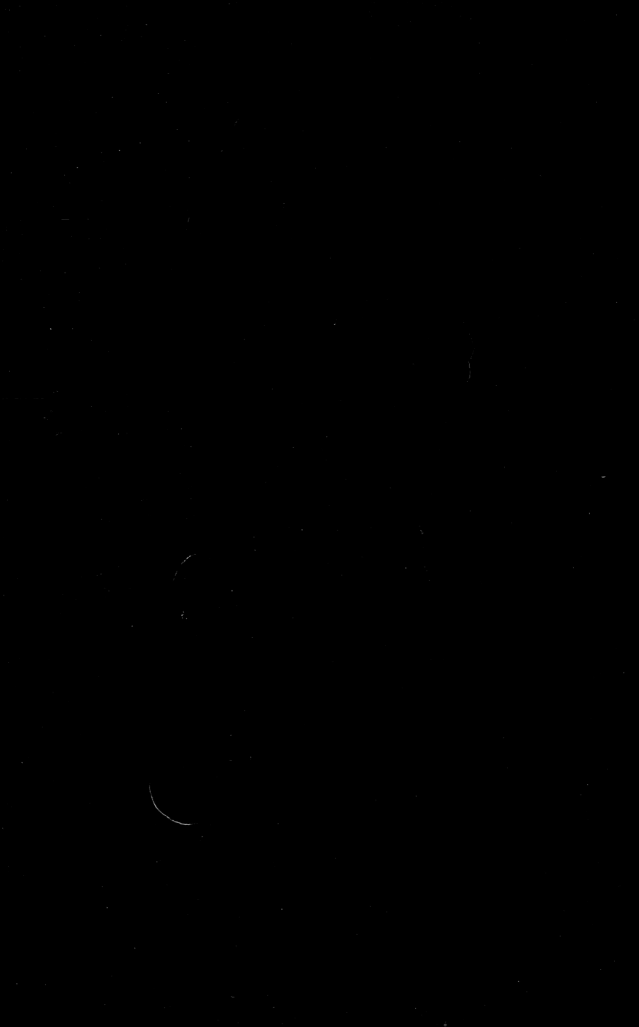

YVES SAINT LAURENT

THE PERFECTION OF STYLE

FLORENCE MÜLLER

EDITED BY FLORENCE MÜLLER AND CHIYO ISHIKAWA

SkiraRizzoli
NEW YORK

Preface

——

Pierre Bergé

President, Fondation Pierre Bergé – Yves Saint Laurent

In 1962, the first fashion show Yves Saint Laurent held under his own name opened with a navy blue wool pea coat worn with a pair of white shantung pants. This article of clothing—a manifesto for his entire body of work—would set the tone for a decade's worth of invention and audacity, during which such garments as the trench coat, the Tuxedo, the safari jacket, the pantsuit, and the jumpsuit would appear on the runway. In just ten years, Yves Saint Laurent revolutionized the fashion world. Garments borrowed from the male wardrobe ended up composing that of the modern woman and forming the foundation of Saint Laurent's distinct style, which—as Mademoiselle Chanel's worthy heir—he would never cease to refine throughout his career.

This immediately recognizable style coincided with the emancipation of women—all women, not only wealthy haute couture customers. In 1966, the creation of the immensely successful SAINT LAURENT *rive gauche*, the first ready-to-wear boutique to bear a couturier's name, paved the way for what has become the fashion we know today. In this respect, Yves Saint Laurent's work has surpassed that of the simple couturier, using an aesthetic perspective to cover social ground.

Created in 2002, the Fondation Pierre Bergé – Yves Saint Laurent holds a unique collection, currently unmatched by any other couture house. From day one, Yves Saint Laurent and I chose to carefully conserve the most important designs along with sketches, photographs, videos, press clippings, and so on. In addition to this initial mission to conserve, we were also concerned with promotion. Remember that this began as early as 1983, when the first exhibition ever devoted to a living couturier and curated by none other than Diana Vreeland opened at the Metropolitan Museum of Art in New York, going on to travel the world.

Previous page:
Yves Saint Laurent preparing his first collection with Victoire Doutreleau, 11, rue Jean-Goujon, Paris, December 1961.

——

Opposite page: Yves Saint Laurent and Pierre Bergé in their apartment, 55, rue de Babylone, Paris, 1982.

The foundation continues to pursue this work today, and I am happy to present the exhibition *Yves Saint Laurent: The Perfection of Style* in Seattle. Some of the designs on display have never before been shown to the American public. I would sincerely like to thank the Seattle Art Museum, which initiated this project, and especially Kimerly Rorschach, the Illsley Ball Nordstrom Director and CEO, and Chiyo Ishikawa, the Susan Brotman Deputy Director for Art and Curator of European Painting and Sculpture. I would equally like to express my gratitude to Florence Müller, who curated this exhibition, and Nathalie Crinière, who has so beautifully displayed everything. I am also very happy that this exhibition has been so enthusiastically received by the Virginia Museum of Fine Arts in Richmond, which will host it in the spring of 2017. My heartfelt thanks go to Alex Nyerges, Director, and Michael Taylor, Chief Curator and Deputy Director for Art and Education.

So what is left of Yves Saint Laurent, nearly fifteen years after the closing of his haute couture house and beyond the many exhibitions devoted to his work? You will discover that to this day, a wonderful heritage still remains, the most important aspect of which is that women—sometimes without even knowing it—continue to wear a little bit of Saint Laurent.

Translated from the French by Angela Krieger.

Director's Foreword

Kimerly Rorschach

Illsley Ball Nordstrom Director and CEO, Seattle Art Museum

The Seattle Art Museum is delighted to present *Yves Saint Laurent: The Perfection of Style*, organized in collaboration with the Fondation Pierre Bergé – Yves Saint Laurent in Paris. Long known as a pioneer in the world of fashion design, Saint Laurent has been the subject of numerous exhibitions around the world, including the Metropolitan Museum of Art's first-ever show devoted to a living designer in 1983. Seattle may not come immediately to mind as a fashion capital of the world, but our city has emerged as an international center of innovation in business, technology, research, and philanthropy, home to such global giants as Microsoft, Starbucks, and Amazon, as well as the Bill & Melinda Gates Foundation and the Allen Institute for Brain Science. Thus it is entirely fitting that an exhibition devoted to one of the world's greatest innovators in design and fashion will find an eager reception in a city that is leading the way into the twenty-first century.

Seattle is also home to a thriving community of artists, architects, designers, and fashion creators, and almost sixty percent of our residents are under the age of forty. Along with style lovers of all ages and those interested in the artist's complex creative process, these young, forward-thinking audiences will find much to inspire them. As Pierre Bergé points out, Saint Laurent invented for women's fashion such enduring trends as the trench coat, the menswear look, the pantsuit, and the jumpsuit, previously unseen but now well-loved staples of women's wardrobes around the world. More than any other designer of his time Saint Laurent also embraced and promoted the concept of ready-to-wear, inspired by the notion that while few women could afford expensive couture clothing, style and fashion could be made available at all price points, an idea embodied today in the mass-market fashion offerings of Zara, H&M, Topshop, and many others. Saint Laurent also

Opposite page: Yves Saint Laurent and models at the American launch of *Opium* perfume on board the *Peking*, New York, September 1978.

influenced the development of women's fashion offerings at major department stores such as Seattle's own Nordstrom, and it is worth recalling that Seattle's Frederick & Nelson department store opened a SAINT LAURENT *rive gauche* boutique in the late 1960s.

The Seattle exhibition will survey the range of Saint Laurent's contributions over a forty-year career while emphasizing his creative process and his stature as an artistic genius, arguably no less inventive and energetic than a Michelangelo or a Picasso. An exhibition of this scope and range is possible only because the Fondation Pierre Bergé – Yves Saint Laurent had the foresight to collect and preserve, from the beginning, the most important garments, as well as sketches, fabric samples, and virtually complete documentation from Saint Laurent's studio and production process. Saint Laurent was also a discerning collector of art. Along with a love of European paintings and decorative arts, his designs show a keen appreciation for the innovations of modern painters such as Pablo Picasso, Georges Braque, Henri Matisse, Piet Mondrian, and American pop artist Tom Wesselmann. The exhibition will illuminate these relationships and how they inspired Saint Laurent's designs.

We are enormously grateful to the Fondation Pierre Bergé – Yves Saint Laurent, and to Pierre Bergé, for partnering with us to produce this splendid exhibition. We wish to thank Director Philippe Mugnier, as well as Olivier Flaviano, Assistant to the Director; Sophie Hovanessian, Advisor to the foundation; Sandrine Tinturier, Head of Conservation; Valérie Mulattieri, Head Exhibition Coordinator/Registrar; Pauline Vidal, Photo and Video Archivist; and members of the foundation's team: Olivier Ségot, Alice Coulon, Domitille Elbé, Lola Fournier, Simon Freschard, Gaëlle Hennion, Laurence Neveu, Joséphine Théry, Célia Thibaud, Leslie Veyrat, and Catherine Zeitoun. In addition, we would like to express our thanks to Anouschka and Hamish Bowles for lending a few carefully selected garments from their personal collections to complement the foundation's holdings.

The guest curator for the exhibition, renowned fashion historian Florence Müller, was responsible for selecting the works in the exhibition and for writing the perceptive text that shapes this book. Her insights about Yves Saint Laurent and his working process and her thorough understanding of the business of fashion enrich every aspect of the exhibition and publication. We are deeply grateful for her contributions.

We also thank Maryse Camelan for bringing the idea of this exhibition to our attention. We are grateful to Nathalie Crinière and Chloé Degaille of Agence NC, Paris, for their warm collaboration and inspired exhibition design.

We are delighted that the exhibition will also be presented at the Virginia Museum of Fine Arts in Richmond, with whom we have collaborated very productively in the past. We extend warm thanks to Alex Nyerges, Director; Michael Taylor, Chief Curator and Deputy Director for Art and Education; and Courtney Burkhardt, Exhibition Projects Coordinator, for their partnership in this endeavor.

As always, it is the Seattle Art Museum's tremendous staff whose excellent work makes this ambitious project possible. Chiyo Ishikawa, SAM's Susan Brotman Deputy Director for Art and Curator of European

Painting and Sculpture, worked with Florence Müller in shaping the curatorial direction for the exhibition and oversaw all aspects of its presentation in Seattle. I am grateful for her passion and wide-ranging knowledge of fashion and style. Key contributions were made by all members of our great team: Zora Hutlova Foy, Deputy Director for Art Administration; Tina Lee, Exhibitions and Publications Manager; Rachel Hsu, Exhibitions Coordinator; Nicholas Dorman, Chief Conservator; Regan Pro, Kayla Skinner, Deputy Director for Education and Public Programs; Paula Tharp, Corporate Relations Officer; Tiffany Tessada, Director of Membership; Linda Rabadi Fair, Director of Individual Giving; Lauren Mellon, Director of Museum Services and Chief Registrar; Leesha Alston, Senior Registrar for Exhibitions; Domenic Morea, Director of Communications; Cindy McKinley, Associate Director of Communications; Chris Manojlovic, Director of Exhibition Design; Paul Martinez, Exhibition Designer; and their talented exhibitions team. Grand exhibitions like this deserve grand opening events. We are enormously grateful to our Director of Special Events, Andrea Burgess Coldwell, and her team for their tireless efforts.

We thank Skira Rizzoli, New York, particularly Margaret Rennolds Chace, Associate Publisher, and Caitlin Leffel, Senior Editor, for their professional and collegial collaboration. We are grateful to Cristina Vasquez for her expert design of this beautiful book.

Support for this ambitious project was provided by generous donors to SAM's Fund for Special Exhibitions – with special thanks to Jeff and Susan Brotman, Barney A. Ebsworth, the Jon and Mary Shirley Foundation, the Bagley and Virginia Wright Foundation, and Ann P. Wyckoff. We are enormously grateful to the exhibition's Presenting Sponsors – Microsoft, Nordstrom, and the Seattle Art Museum Supporters (SAMS). Special thanks also to SAM's Official Airline – Delta Air Lines. Additional support for the exhibition was provided by the many generous contributors to the SAM Fund.

This exhibition takes place at a moment when the practice of haute couture bears little resemblance to what it was in Saint Laurent's day—the world described in this book. This is also a time of change for the Fondation Pierre Bergé – Yves Saint Laurent. The foundation presents exhibitions of Saint Laurent's work all over the world, continuing what the couture house started as early as 1983. Now, besides continuing to build its collection, the foundation also dedicates its efforts to opening two museums devoted to the designer, where visitors can see garments and documents from its collection. In 2017 the Musée Yves Saint Laurent Marrakech will open in the city that first captivated Saint Laurent and Pierre Bergé in 1966, whereas the Musée Yves Saint Laurent Paris will open at 5, avenue Marceau, in the building that housed the couture operation from 1974 to 2002, and where the public will be able to visit the designer's studio. As the foundation moves into this next chapter in its history, we are thrilled to have the opportunity to present Saint Laurent's groundbreaking achievements to new audiences in the United States. Over one hundred garments, some of them newly acquired and never before exhibited, offer an unforgettable reminder of Saint Laurent's genius and show how he achieved a true perfection of style.

Nan Kempner wearing
a navy crepe de chine
dress and an embroidered
jacket, Spring-Summer
haute couture collection 1972.
Vogue U.S., January 1974.

YSL: The Perfection of Style

Reflecting on his creative evolution in 1982, Yves Saint Laurent declared, "I am no longer concerned with sensation and innovation, but with the perfection of my style."[1] Based on the couturier's belief that the power of style reaches well beyond the ephemeral fluctuations of fashion, Saint Laurent's career is now considered his oeuvre. As such, his body of work has become the subject of exhibitions in the world's most important museums as they pay homage to the universal and timeless qualities of the Saint Laurent style. This unique and comprehensive installation, comparable to that of an artist, has found a perfect home in a vital institution such as the Seattle Art Museum.

This exhibition signals a new phase in the exploration of Saint Laurent's mythic style—a style that continues to influence contemporary design. Featuring collections from the Fondation Pierre Bergé – Yves Saint Laurent, *The Perfection of Style* includes many previously unseen documents as well as recent acquisitions of iconic styles in the history of fashion. More than one hundred complete outfits provide intimate insight into the couturier's personality (the topic of two recently released biopics). Numerous documents accompany the haute couture and ready-to-wear SAINT LAURENT *rive gauche* creations. Collection boards featuring sketches from every Saint Laurent show held between 1962 and 2002 retrace forty years of the *maison de couture*'s history. Numerous photographs, films, magazines, drawings, and production documents offer a behind-the-scenes look into the creative workings of the fashion house and the private life of the couturier. Official and personal portraits of Yves Saint Laurent reveal how his own style echoed the remarkable look he designed for the men and women of his time. Meticulously conserved documents will shed new light on the couturier's oeuvre—including drawings from his adolescence and research sketches from his early days as Christian Dior's assistant. And, for the first time, American viewers will discover his *maison de couture* crafted out of cut paper when he was a young boy. Eleven carefully selected dolls and more than four hundred outfits and one hundred miniature accessories created between 1953 and 1955 offer a fascinating look at the unique destiny of the young prodigy who would become one of the greatest couturiers of all time.

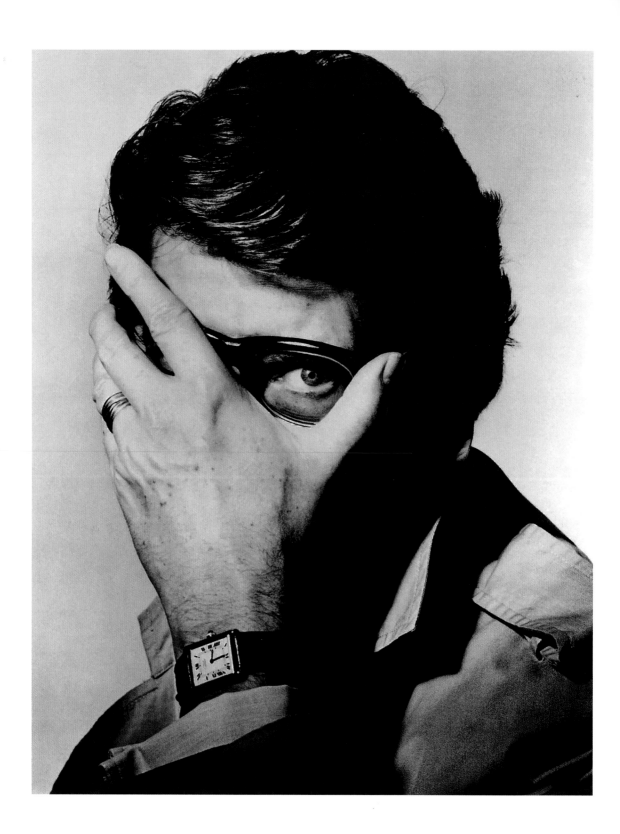

Yves Saint Laurent, 1983.

"My weapon is the perspective in which I see my society."

Yves Saint Laurent

The Style of Now

The 1960s, a decade dominated by avant-garde experiences and research in the fields of art, music, film, and design, signaled the moment when society crossed the threshold into modernity. Saint Laurent would accomplish the same in the field of fashion. Society was reinventing itself, establishing new sets of values; but despite the revolutionary momentum, Saint Laurent, in singular fashion, would make no sacrifice for the sake of arbitrary novelty. Unencumbered by nostalgia like many of his elders, such as Pierre Balmain or Christian Dior, or obsessed with the future like his contemporaries André Courrèges, Pierre Cardin, and Paco Rabanne, Saint Laurent embraced the present. His message was clear: women do not need to focus on the fashions of yesterday or tomorrow—they need to dress for today. He was also keenly aware of the hedonism driving the times: this younger generation wanted everything and wanted it right away. Speed, instant gratification, self-fulfillment: these were the new lifestyle codes. Young people sought immediate pleasure, sexual liberation, and freedom from the constraints of the past. Like James Dean, Françoise Sagan, and Françoise Hardy, Saint Laurent embodied a mix of melancholy and lust for life, of fragility and rebellion, of existential angst and unbridled ambition; this natural predisposition allowed him to channel angst and sadness into an infinite source of creativity. Throughout his life, he would retain the sharp acuity of the hypersensitive. Contributing to the advancement of modernity, style replaced fashion and modern women began expressing themselves through their sartorial choices. Unlike Dior or Cristóbal Balenciaga, who had fiercely guarded their private lives, Saint Laurent, imbued with natural charisma, was an instant darling of the media, who elevated him to the status of a rock star. He was the master organizer of the haute couture fashion world that would dominate the social scene. Public and private lives converged as reality and discourse became one. Thrilled to follow such an exhilarating personality, the media were ever-present. His entourage included the most celebrated personalities of the time, such as Catherine Deneuve, Mick and Bianca Jagger, Maria Callas, Rudolf Nureyev, Andy Warhol, and David Hockney. As the first pop culture couturier, Saint Laurent paved the way for the synergy of minor and

Opposite page: Daytime dress worn by Willy van Rooy, Spring-Summer 1971 haute couture collection. *Elle,* March 1971.

———

Next page: Yves Saint Laurent, 1968.

major art forms, of elite and popular culture. The Saint Laurent style appealed to everyone, from the Baroness Rothschild to Liza Minnelli, from Nan Kempner to Brigitte Bardot, from Marella Agnelli to Jane Birkin. It would transform him from a great designer into a mythic figure able to transcend the fleeting nature of fashion. His own legacy was built over time by critics and reviewers and by the creation of a cultural heritage that would serve fashion worshippers from all over the world. Well before today's media coverage and the fashion world's star system of the 1990s and 2000s, Saint Laurent had already become the stuff of legend.

THE PRODIGAL CHILD

"Genius is finding childhood again. I have been lucky enough to realize all of my childhood dreams," Saint Laurent confided to Catherine Deneuve.[1] His mother's blue eyes and the magic of a puppet theater were among his cherished childhood memories. Originally from Alsace, the family had settled in Oran, Algeria. One of his forefathers was the Baron de Mauvières, Napoleon's solicitor (years later, Yves Saint Laurent would inherit his desk). In the large house situated at 11, rue de Stora, Yves lived with his father, a corporate insurer, his beautiful mother and two sisters, Michèle and Brigitte, and an aunt and uncle and their two children, Patrice and Catherine. His was a wonderful and enchanted childhood. As a good student who never disappointed his parents, he enjoyed a great deal of freedom. Each evening, the children would gather around him in a tiny room located between the ground and second floors. In this space, he invented a magical world; it was also a place where he could escape from a reality that he was not yet prepared to share with his family. He had become a target of bullying by his schoolmates at the Collège du Sacré-Coeur—they suspected he was a homosexual. "I took refuge in an imaginary, solitary world, where I felt safe," he revealed years later.[2] In this fantasy world, he could be an orchestra conductor, a film director, an interior designer, or a couturier. The other children, who alternated roles as actors or audience, adored him. He would tell them fantastic stories of wild sea journeys, of princesses and castles lit by arm-bearing torches that came out of the walls—even then, he was acknowledging Jean Cocteau. He acted out entire plays, running back and forth on a wooden board balanced over two bricks. He cut out silhouettes of famous models Bettina and Suzy Parker from fashion magazines and created entire outfits for them made of paper. He used the dolls to put on a fashion show for his sisters, who received invitations addressed to "Madame la Baronne" or "Madame la Comtesse." He prepared programs that featured the names of actual suppliers to the haute couture trade, such as

Yves Saint Laurent and
his mother, Lucienne, in Oran,
Algeria, in the early 1940s.

Bianchini-Férier, Abraham, Bucol, Hurel, Staron, and Brossin de Méré, and included bootmaker Perugia, the hairdresser Carita, and makeup by Elizabeth Arden. Michèle and Brigitte would make their selections, place their orders, and record their choices in small notebooks. Saint Laurent had even imagined a prêt-à-porter collection, La Boutique d'Y.M.S.L. It was a dress rehearsal for his destiny as an adult, carried out with complete confidence in his good fortune. At the age of nine, he had announced to his bemused family, "One day, my name will appear in lights on the Champs-Élysées."[3]

During his adolescence, Saint Laurent's parents offered him an even larger refuge, a garage in their villa in Trouville, the trendy beach resort near Oran. Transformed into a nightclub and decorated with figures of jazz dancers, the former garage soon became a party space. Saint Laurent invited all his friends, and all the pretty girls were in love with him. Fashion became a clear career choice. Confident in his ability to draw, in 1953 he submitted sketches to the Woolmark Prize competition sponsored by the International Wool Secretariat. He won that year, and the year following. He went to Paris both times to receive his prize, and the second year he met a co-winner, Karl Lagerfeld. Over the next twenty years, Saint Laurent and Lagerfeld shared the same group of friends, attended the same parties, and enjoyed everything Paris had to offer.

With his mother at his side, Saint Laurent set off to conquer the world of fashion. Shy but determined and brimming with ambition, he aimed for the top: *Vogue* and Christian Dior. Thanks to a letter of introduction from his father, Saint Laurent met Michel de Brunhoff, the powerful editor in chief of *Vogue Paris* and Edmonde Charles-Roux, the magazine's future editor in chief. Saint Laurent followed Brunhoff's advice, obtaining his baccalaureate degree and then pursuing his studies at the École chambre syndicale de la couture. After a vacation in Oran, Saint Laurent returned to Paris in 1955 and showed Brunhoff fifty of his drawings. In a later letter to Charles-Roux, Brunhoff wrote that twenty of the drawings could have come from Dior himself. Brunhoff decided to personally introduce the young prodigy to Christian Dior, who hired him on the spot as an assistant. The amazing journey had begun.

Program for a collection
created by Yves Saint Laurent
for his paper dolls, 1953–1954.

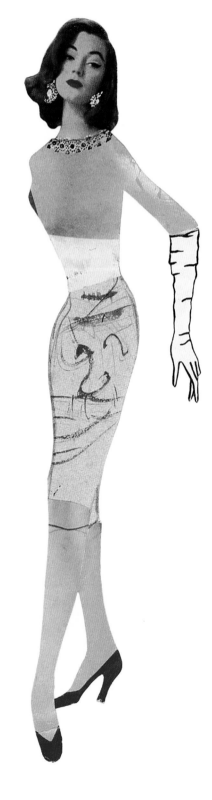

"Ivy" doll with four outfits
from her wardrobe,
1953–1954. Paper doll cut out
of a magazine and glued onto
cardboard. Garments made
of paper cutouts, ink,
watercolor, and gouache.

Yves Saint Laurent and Karl
Lagerfeld at the International
Wool Secretariat awards,
Paris, November 1954.

THE LITTLE PRINCE OF FASHION

Starting with the Winter 1955 collection, Dior, the world's most celebrated couturier, began to include his young assistant's designs in the collections. A black dress draped with a white scarf caused a sensation when it appeared in the now iconic photograph by Richard Avedon, Dovima with Elephants. But Christian Dior's sudden death in 1957 would bring up the delicate matter of succession. Though Dior had chosen Saint Laurent to succeed him, Marcel Boussac, the *maison*'s owner, wondered how a twenty-one-year-old could possibly take over what had become the premier address in French luxury. But Saint Laurent was hired and presented his first collection for Summer 1958. Backstage, Yves Saint Laurent wore a sprig of lily of the valley in his buttonhole—it was Christian Dior's favorite good-luck charm. It would bring him luck as well: the *Trapeze* collection was met with thunderous applause. Instant stardom followed as the couturier appeared on the cover of *Paris Match* with models Bettina and Christine. The painter Bernard Buffet drew one of Saint Laurent's dresses for the cover of *L'Express*. *Elle* magazine published an article called "Portrait of a young man at the helm of an empire" and quoted the determined designer: "No, I am not afraid of the great responsibility that has fallen to me."[4] The magazine was enthralled by the newness of the *Trapeze* line and its silhouettes "that are free, light, less bourgeois [...] that fall straight or flared like little girls' dresses ..."[5] "I never saw a better Dior collection," raved Eugenia Sheppard while the young designer blew kisses from the *maison*'s balcony to those who came to congratulate him. Everyone in the salon was in tears. "The young man on the flying trapeze" was crowned "Little Prince of Fashion."[6]

The *Trapeze* line launched the fashion of the 1960s. Girlish dresses, free of waistlines, liberated the body from the constraints of clothing. One year later, in his Summer 1959 collection, Saint Laurent declared, "Line has been sacrificed to the benefit of style," and radically turned away from the system put in place by his mentor, Dior.[7] No more imposed rules about shape, proportion, and skirt length—the obsession of magazines and women for so long. It was now all about style! For his third collection, Saint Laurent went even further: leather—the kind worn by French *blousons noirs* and American bikers, made a startling appearance in the hushed salons of avenue Montaigne. Models, wearing simple knitted caps and dressed all in black, wore looks whose names evoked the heroes of the youth culture, Rebelle, Jazz, Avant-Garde, Marilyn, Lolita, *Un tramway nommé Désir* (A Streetcar Named Desire), *À bout de souffle* (Breathless), Dolce Vita. The "Chicago" leather jacket was seen by the press as the emblem of the stylistic revolution that would send the *maison*'s clientele running. Drafted into the army, Saint Laurent took a leave of absence but was ultimately declared unfit for service. He soon fell into a deep depression. The House of Dior did not renew his contract.

Oposite page: "Chicago" daytime ensemble, Fall-Winter 1960 *Yves Saint Laurent for Christian Dior* haute couture collection. Jacket of black patent crocodile, trimmed with black mink; skirt of black bouclé wool.

Yves Saint Laurent, 1957.

Next page: "Elephant blanc" short evening dress, Spring-Summer 1958 *Yves Saint Laurent for Christian Dior* haute couture collection, known as the *Trapeze* collection. Trapeze dress of white tulle embroidered with silver metallic thread and rhinestones.

"Dahlia" end-of-day dress,
Spring-Summer 1959 *Yves
Saint Laurent for Christian Dior*
haute couture collection.
Flame-red warp-print taffeta
dress with orange floral
pattern, wrap-style bodice,
large double-looped bow
on front of waist, and raised
bubble skirt.

Next page: "Dahlia" end-of-
day dress (detail).

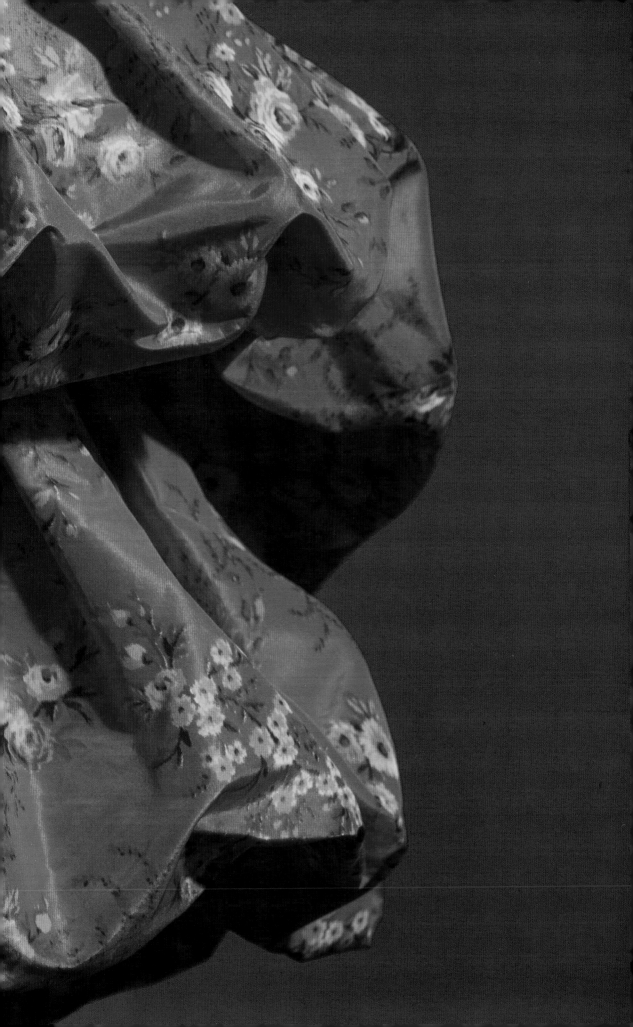

THE BEATNIK COUTURIER

Saint Laurent met Pierre Bergé after the *Trapeze* show. They would remain together from then on and experience the biggest success story in the history of fashion. When their new fashion house opened its doors in 1962, each man had his role: Yves was the artist and Pierre the businessman. Pierre developed a business model that was as unique as his partner and one that is still studied in marketing and fashion schools. Bergé liked to describe himself as a manager: "I don't really like doing business. I've never been good with figures. Perhaps I am a frustrated artist. I don't have a businessman's instincts. And I try not to. But I never stopped having fun."[8] With Bergé running the business and managing the staff and the media, Saint Laurent could devote himself exclusively to his creative work. Evenings out were spent with Pierre, Saint Laurent's older sister Michèle, and Victoire Doutreleau, the director of couture. The two young women always wore dresses designed by Saint Laurent. Oftentimes, the couturier worked alone at night in the empty *maison*—the cleaning staff would wake him at 6:00 a.m. Novelist Dino Buzzati, who knew Saint Laurent during those years, did not find him "in the least bit dangerous or mysterious. In fact, his thoughtful and pale expression gave him a terribly romantic look. Mostly, he seemed serious and well-mannered, a perfect aristocrat."[9]

The first collection was presented on January 29, 1962, at 30 bis, rue Spontini, in the townhouse that once belonged to painter Jean-Louis Forain, the famous political satirist of the Belle Époque. The traditional world of haute couture was changing. Saint Laurent was no longer designing just for the elite but for the modern independent woman as well. His collections drew their inspiration from street life and the creative excitement of pop culture. According to *Women's Wear Daily*'s John Fairchild, "This guy is the only designer in Paris who really belongs to the sixties because he's part of the world around him and therefore understands it."[10] Saint Laurent was the first to explore the interaction between creative style and street life—one is inspired by the other and returns the favor with a style-amplified image. You no longer needed to be rich to have style.

Opposite page: French singer Françoise Hardy wearing the first Tuxedo, Fall-Winter 1966 SAINT LAURENT *rive gauche* collection.

First Yves Saint Laurent haute
couture show, January 29, 1962.
30 bis, rue Spontini, Paris.

————

Opposite Page: Yves Saint
Laurent in the wings of his
first haute couture show,
January 29, 1962. 30 bis, rue
Spontini, Paris.

Tuxedo dress, Fall-Winter
1966 haute couture collection.
Black woolen dress with
flounced bib and white organdy cuffs; black patent leather
belt with gold metal buckle.
Tuxedo dress (detail).

A chasm was growing between haute couture clients and this new streetwise fashion. When Saint Laurent first presented the "Le Smoking" Tuxedo in 1966, the reception was luke-warm—his clients could not imagine wearing it in place of an evening gown. Still, Saint Laurent maintained that the formal ways of the past had become obsolete. (Pierre Bergé recalled Saint Laurent comparing women in formal attire to "upholstered chairs"!)[11] Believing that haute couture was no longer a barometer of modernity, Saint Laurent and Bergé enthusiastically developed their ready-to-wear concept by launching the SAINT LAURENT *rive gauche* label. A pioneer in luxury ready-to-wear, the brand succeeded beyond their wildest expectations, enjoying worldwide acclaim. The Tuxedo caused a shopping frenzy in the brand's first boutique, which opened on rue de Tournon in 1966. Once Françoise Hardy wore it to an event in the United States, any woman who dared to follow her example was sure to cause a sensation. The Tuxedo was the "it" item of 1966. With the foundation of his style now firmly in place, Saint Laurent proclaimed, "I invented its past, I gave it a future and it will endure well after my death."[12] He provoked the press further, declaring that haute couture was dead.

The shy young man in the black tie had evolved into a longhaired beatnik couturier. He exemplified the synchronicity between appearance and lifestyle. During that same period, Yves and Pierre visited Morocco and bought Dar el-Hanch—House of the Serpent—in the Marrakech medina. There, hair blowing in the wind, wearing jeans, a T-shirt, sandals or barefoot, Saint Laurent rediscovered the pleasures of North Africa. He was seduced by the chic bohemian lifestyle, easy, free of conventions, living *à l'orientale*. His group of friends included artists, the "beautiful people," the young millionaires Paul and Talitha Getty, Mick and Bianca Jagger, interior designer Bill Willis, the Dreamachine inventor Brion Gysin, designer Fernando Sánchez, and the Countess Charles de Breteuil. And, of course, *"les jolies filles,"* the beautiful women who were his closest friends and who exemplified the many different and inspiring facets of a modern woman: Betty Catroux, Loulou de La Falaise, and Paloma Picasso. In Paris, he spent time with Andy Warhol, his alter ego in the world of contemporary art. Saint Laurent met Warhol in 1970 during the shooting of *L'Amour*, the experimental film directed by Warhol, Paul Morrissey, and other members of the Factory. Karl Lagerfeld played one of the principal roles in this underground film, which was shot in his Paris apartment. Saint Laurent appears several times in Warhol's *Factory Diaries* between 1971 and 1974, the period during which Warhol made several portraits of the couturier.

Opposite page: Yves Saint Laurent at the souk, Marrakech, 1972. *W,* April 1972.

Next page: Daytime ensemble worn by Mounia, Fall-Winter 1980 SAINT LAURENT *rive gauche* collection, Paris.

THE CELEBRITY COUTURIER

During the 1970s, Saint Laurent's status went from fashionable couturier to superstar on a par with Mick Jagger or David Bowie. At the time, some rock stars gave performances that bordered on the extreme in a kind of onstage catharsis. Saint Laurent would do the same. As if his subjective style demanded a personal sacrifice, he would shock the public with his own nudity. In November 1971, to promote his men's fragrance launched three years earlier, he released a photograph of himself in the nude shot by Jeanloup Sieff. Anticipating the reaction, Bergé placed it in just a few magazines: *Vogue Paris*, *Paris Match*, *L'Express*, and *Le Nouvel Observateur*. For the next week, the phone rang incessantly while the media clamored for the photograph, offering to publish it free of charge. Speaking to the press, Saint Laurent insisted, "There's no aesthetic purpose, no *sous-entendu* (innuendo). It came naturally [. . .] I find it amusing [. . .] I wanted to shock."[13] Acknowledging the scandal, Saint Laurent claimed to have diminished the shock factor by giving the image a biblical feel. But French designers were outraged by the bold ad that relegated them further into the shadows. Pierre Balmain, the only good sport among them, commented that "Saint Laurent was lucky to be still able to pull off such a gesture."[14] The portrait, one of the most memorable photographs of the seventies, marks a turning point in the representation of masculinity. Far from the usual depiction of the all-powerful male figure, the image reveals man's feminine side—in this case, a man who, despite the taboos, never denied his homosexuality.

Having experienced the thrill of scandal, Saint Laurent would create them again and again over the next ten years. The launch of his 1971 summer collection was met with indignation on the part of the critics. With hindsight, it is difficult to understand how such a beautifully conceived and impeccably cut collection could have elicited such loathing from the press. The scandal erupted because the show reawakened the tragic and shameful memories of the German occupation. But, in truth, it was the reference to the wartime *demimondaines* that hit a nerve. Saint Laurent disagreed, claiming that the collection ". . . was the result of a memory. During the war, I was in Oran, and women at that time had a special kind of seductive ability, perhaps because of the worrisome times, the men, the dreams, the heroism. My mother had gone out one evening wearing a short black crepe dress with very squared shoulders and long sleeves, with a V neck, draped under the bust, carrying an enormous bouquet of poppies, cornflowers and daisies. [. . .] And 1971 was also when I first met Paloma Picasso, who was very ahead of her time in fashion. That particular day she was wearing a dress and a hat from the 1940s that had belonged to her mother. Her lips were a deep shade of red. It shocked me."[15] Saint Laurent also introduced the important retro movement and anticipated the revival of a more sophisticated look. The younger generation, tired of the casual hippie style, was ready for something new.

Yves Saint Laurent posing
for the advertisement of his
first eau de toilette, *Pour
Homme*, 1971.

Opposite page: Short evening dress worn by Anjelica Huston, Spring-Summer 1971 haute couture collection. *Vogue Italia,* June 1971.

Bianca Perez wearing an Yves Saint Laurent suit for her wedding with Mick Jagger in Saint-Tropez, May 12, 1971.

Yves Saint Laurent: The Perfection of Style · The Style of Now

nother seismic moment occurred in 1976 when the collection named *Opera-Ballets Russes* celebrated haute couture
and the return to elegance. Expensive, well-cut clothes made
from luxurious fabrics were seen as the reflection of an old caste system
and had been rejected during the May 1968 anti-establishment unrest.
But ten years after the protests, Saint Laurent could sense a shift that
favored a return to haute couture and sophistication. The opera and its
old-fashioned ambiance was the perfect setting for its reinvention. For
some time, audiences had given up the once-mandatory evening attire in
favor of a more casual style. This show would reintroduce the dress and
manners of society life when people would dress to the nines. Featuring
light slip dresses and soft Russian-style blouses, the new designs were
still less constricting than the old-fashioned garments.

   Five years in the making, *Opium* perfume was launched in 1977.
The fragrance's debut caused a huge scandal because its name alluded
to the drug epidemic afflicting many young people in the United States.
The firm Charles of the Ritz, which owned Parfums Saint Laurent,
had to fend off American anti-drug coalitions as well as the Chinese-
American community. The famous American fashion critic André Leon
Talley coined the term "The Opium Wars," while the *New York Times*
reported on the "Opium Battle." Following heated negotiations, the
advertising campaign slogan for the United States was changed from
"For women who give themselves to Saint Laurent" to "For women
who adore Saint Laurent." Meanwhile, the designer claimed he never
intended to cause a scandal, that the name was a reference to the 1920s
and the early days of modernity when the influence of Orientalism had
revolutionized Western art. "Byron and Delacroix, Rimbaud, Baudelaire,
they all understood the exotic beauty of the Orient without having to
travel there," he told André Leon Talley.[16] He wanted to capture the
essence of a contemporary, romantic, sensual, and provocative woman.
Never had the launch of a perfume caused so much ink to flow. Marina
Schiano and Giorgio di Sant'Angelo organized the brilliantly decadent
party held in 1978 aboard the *Peking*, a large sailboat docked in New
York. An imposing bronze Buddha presided over the disco dance floor
decorated with hundreds of orchids. Chinese acrobats added to the
evening's authenticity while cushions strewn everywhere recalled wild

Opposite page: Evening gown designed for the singer and actress Jane Birkin for the Proust Ball given by Marie-Hélène de Rothschild in December 1971. Ivory silk crepe ball gown with train, guipure lace on the back and sleeves; ivory silk satin belt forming a pouf at the back.

Singer and actress Jane Birkin wearing an evening gown designed for the Proust Ball, December 1971.

nights in Marrakech. The celebration moved on to Studio 54, where a breakfast of champagne and omelets was served in the early morning hours. The who's who of New York was there, greeted by a beaming Saint Laurent surrounded by his entourage of opulently dressed top models. Guests included Mikhail Baryshnikov, Jacqueline Onassis, Lynn Wyatt, the Kissingers, the Rockefellers, several Kennedys, Andy Warhol, Cher, Faye Dunaway, Warren Beatty, Truman Capote, and top American designers Donna Karan, Oscar de la Renta, Calvin Klein, Pauline Trigère, Bill Blass, and Mary McFadden, as well as Gianni Versace, Zandra Rhodes, Grace Jones, and Halston, who was seen "sniffing" drops of opium from the inside of his wrist. "Yves didn't offer us any opium!" exclaimed Diana Vreeland, seated on a case of champagne and enjoying some caviar.[17] For Allan Mottus, a beauty industry analyst, the evening was the realization of the designer's American dream: "The Saint Laurent party introduced Saint Laurent to the ordinary people of America," he commented.[18] The commercial success was immediate, one of the most spectacular in the history of perfume. Stores sold out of *Opium* within three or four days.

The 1970s were a time of success and scandal as Saint Laurent was caught up in a whirlwind of celebrations: jet-set parties, the Proust Ball at the Château de Ferrières, and Rothschild balls held at the Hôtel Lambert alternated with disco nights at the Palace in Paris or Studio 54 in New York. Saint Laurent was drawn to the decadent mood so well captured in Luchino Visconti's films such as *Il gattopardo* (*The Leopard*, 1963) or *La caduta degli dei* (*The Damned*, 1969)—he was entranced by Helmut Berger's steamy charm. Drifting from party to party with his friend Betty Catroux, Saint Laurent began to lose touch with the reality of everyday life. Pierre Bergé and Betty's husband, François Catroux, did their best to act as "parents" and reign in their unruly "children." But Saint Laurent, who did not have a typical childhood, refused to grow up. His antidote to ennui was satisfying his most outlandish desires. He wanted to experience everything "intensely" but ended up enmeshed in dangerous sexual escapades and artificial paradises. In the late 1970s, Saint Laurent and Betty Catroux entered a rehabilitation program but the couturier would never be completely free of his inner demons.

Opposite page: Evening gown, Spring-Summer 1985 haute couture collection. Red silk crepe: plunging v-neck down middle front, draped at the hips.

$1.50 • NOVEMBER 28, 1983

ALL ABOUT YVES
The Costume Institute Celebrates Saint Laurent

New York

*Yves Saint Laurent
with his 'Picasso'
evening dress, 1979–80*

Yves Saint Laurent posing
next to a short evening dress,
from *Homage to Diaghilev
and Picasso,* Fall-Winter 1979
haute couture collection.
"All About Yves," *New York*,
November 28, 1983.

A LIVING LEGEND

From the 1980s until the *maison de couture*'s closing, every fact about or move by the couturier contributed to the creation of his mythic persona. The main credo, orchestrated with Pierre Bergé, was one of generosity and "democracy." The world of haute couture was no longer restricted to an elite but opened to a wider audience. Media coverage of certain key moments allowed the public to enter the couturier's private world as they would an enchanted castle. The first such event was the large retrospective exhibition, celebrating twenty-five years of creation, organized by Diana Vreeland at the Metropolitan Museum of Art in New York in 1983. It was the first time that a living couturier was the subject of a show in a museum. Saint Laurent was only forty-seven years old and about to see his oeuvre recognized by one of the most prestigious institutions in the world. According to Vreeland, the exemplary nature of Saint Laurent's style justified her choice: "Saint Laurent has his ear to the street, he understands that scene, its rhythm and how it wants to be portrayed; he addresses its needs, which are also his own, because he lives in the present, according to his own feelings, his own intuition."[19] The spectacular opening was followed by an avalanche of press glorifying the couturier. The celebrity-studded guests were treated to a dazzling evening and dinner served in the Metropolitan Museum's grand space housing the Temple of Dendur. Chamber music, champagne, tuxedos, and stunning evening gowns were the order of the night. Catherine Deneuve, Roland Petit and Zizi Jeanmaire, Brooke Shields, Baron de Rothschild, Henry Kissinger, and other celebrities drew attention but not as much as the two hundred haute couture figures placed among the masterpieces that covered the walls of galleries filled with perfume and the sounds of Edith Piaf. "It felt more like being in a glamorous closet than in a museum . . ." wrote the reporter from *Libération*.[20] A million visitors pressed into the Costume Institute's rooms to view the motionless fashion show before the exhibit began its worldwide tour, going to Beijing, Paris, Moscow, and, at the invitation of Raisa Gorbachev, to the Hermitage Museum in Saint Petersburg. A stone's throw from the galleries housing the famous Rembrandt paintings, Yves Saint Laurent's dresses created their own dreamlike setting. Recounting the evening to Hélène de Turckheim, Pierre Bergé said, "It was as if you were attending a ball."[21] It was a moment that perhaps foreshadowed Russia's imminent opening to the West.

As *Opium* had done a few years earlier, the 1983 launch of *Paris* perfume triggered protracted negotiations because of its name. Since the name of the French capital could not be attributed to a commercial object, the perfume would have to change its name. Instead of *Paris*, the fragrance was called *Paris d'Yves Saint Laurent*. Created by Sophia Grojsman, a rose specialist, the perfume celebrated the couturier's favorite city. The bottle of perfume was unveiled during the finale of the Winter 1983 fashion show by the model Mounia, who wore a tunic made of bird of paradise plumes—a nod to the legendary Josephine Baker (the star of *La Revue Nègre*, and who sang a 1920s song with the lyrics "J'ai deux amours, mon pays et Paris" (I have two loves, my country and Paris). Six hundred guests attended a reception in the garden of the Hotel InterContinental. Surrounded by hundreds of roses, Saint Laurent fielded questions from the press, flanked by the brunette Paloma Picasso and the blonde Catherine Deneuve, the perfume's muse.

Another global milestone was reached in 1992, this time in Seville, where Saint Laurent's iconic styles were shown in a fashion retrospective at Expo 92. The French pavilion hostesses wore elegant gray pantsuits designed by Saint Laurent. The 1998 World Cup soccer final marked another breakthrough moment in the couturier's life, offering him the opportunity to present haute couture to a truly global audience. In the past, fearing their styles would be copied, designers were wary of the media and sought to exercise complete control over any photographs taken during a fashion show. Saint Laurent took the opposite view: knowing that one could not control the dissemination of ideas and images, he supported the idea of global sharing. He organized an outsized retrospective fashion show at the *Stade de France*. Stunned fans and viewers from all over the world watched three hundred models parade around the stadium to the music of Ravel's "Boléro," accompanied by one hundred percussionists. The *International Herald Tribune* headline read: "YSL Propels French Fashion into the TV Age." Suzy Menkes added that the show "not only made fashion history as an event watched by an estimated billion television spectators. It also marked a rite of passage for French fashion."[22]

But all the accolades could not save the couturier from a slow and irreversible descent into the abyss of depression. Success could no longer guarantee happiness or serve as an antidote to his fears and anxiety. From this moment forward, the couturier retreated from the world. For several years, work was his only passion, but in a moving speech given on January 7, 2002, the couturier announced his decision to retire from haute couture. One last retrospective show, at the Centre Pompidou, marked the end of forty years of creation. With somber staging by Pierre Bergé, the *maison de couture*'s final act struck many as the death knell of a world dedicated to creative freedom. In a note to Saint Laurent, Anna Wintour wrote: "All my congratulations for everything you have achieved and for always being a great fashion leader, never a follower."[23]

Opposite page: Mounia as the bride at the end of a fashion show, holding a bottle of *Paris* perfume, Fall-Winter, 1983. Hotel InterContinental, Paris.

Next page: Yves Saint Laurent surrounded by Laetitia Casta, Catherine Deneuve, and his models, all wearing YSL tuxedos, at the end of his forty-year retrospective fashion show at the Centre Pompidou, Paris, January 22, 2002.

The first Tuxedo, Fall-Winter
1966 SAINT LAURENT
rive gauche collection.
Marie Claire (France),
September 1966.

"I am not interested in beauty. I am only interested in shock and seduction."

Yves Saint Laurent

A Liberated Style

With his haute couture line and SAINT LAURENT *rive gauche* label—the pioneer of luxury ready-to-wear—Yves Saint Laurent liberated the world of fashion. He would invent a look that suited the contemporary woman and reflected her newfound status in society. Saint Laurent dismissed the conventions and restrictions that anchored fashion to the past. His trousers, pullovers, pantsuits, and day-to-night fashions would anticipate the events of May 1968. Three main concepts were the focus of his attention: eliminating the "total outfit," gender issues, and the appeal of originality.

EXPRESSING ONESELF

All three concepts converged on the notion of the individual within society. As of the 1960s, an individual could exercise his or her right to freedom regardless of the structures that once restricted him or her to a group such as family, religion, or occupation. A civilization that had been centered on the idea of collectivity was now at odds with the new order of a society founded on individual accomplishment. Within the traditional system, clothing was dictated by its function or by one's affiliation to a group. Members of the middle class, workmen, or farmers could identify each other by their clothing. Eveningwear or Sunday clothes were different from day or work clothes. Clothing was an especially visible symbol of any attempt to climb up the social hierarchy. This system began to crumble during the events of 1968, and Saint Laurent, sensing the impending shift, was quick to react. He addressed the void left by the renunciation of traditional fashion with the launch of SAINT LAURENT *rive gauche*. Instead of wearing precisely matched outfits, women were free to choose whatever they wanted: the wide variety of items, the diversity of shapes, and extensive range of colors allowed women of all ages and circumstances to express their individuality. Loulou de La Falaise, who lived by that rule, would choose a "look" rather than an "outfit." "An outfit," she believed, "was something that had been determined earlier, whereas a look was an idea."[1]

Moreover, the younger generation had adopted jeans and T-shirts as a sign of belonging to a more egalitarian society—haute couture being seen as a symbol of inequality. "Cool" had replaced "tasteful." Saint Laurent altered the concept of haute couture, creating styles that were easier to wear. "Attitude" replaced "well dressed."

Opposite Page: Wedding dress, Fall-Winter 1970 haute couture collection. Multicolored silk velvet coat with appliqué letters forming the words "LOVE ME FOREVER" (front) and "OR NEVER" (back) and shapes (heart, stars, and a cloud), all in multicolored silk satin.

Nex page:
Wedding dress (detail).

THE PARADOX OF STYLE

During the 1930s, inspired by the Surrealists, Elsa Schiaparelli sought intentionally to shock the bourgeoisie with her provocatively themed collections. Saint Laurent would go further still: "What I want to do is to shock people, force them to think," he said.[2] Not satisfied with merely the bizarre or the eccentric, he pushed provocation into even more complex and subtly paradoxical territories through impossible pairings, improbable juxtapositions, and unnatural associations. Starting with his first collection, he combined the symbols of leisure and work. He appropriated utilitarian clothes for haute couture. The sailor's pea jacket was the first such item to be introduced in the Summer 1962 collection. Why a pea jacket? Because it was authentic—a garment made to withstand the sea, the cold, the rain, and all of nature's unexpected whims. Made of heavy wool, double-breasted with a stand-up collar, the pea jacket was a sailor's protective cocoon. Saint Laurent wore one with a sailor's cap when he took long walks. When he realized that young people were flocking to army surplus stores to buy pea jackets, he decided to make one for women. By urbanizing a symbol of courageous and bold masculinity, he gave the coat extra appeal in the charm of a uniform instead of the frivolity of adornment. He retained the original coat's qualities—sturdiness, protection, and comfort as well as its full cut—but added a "twist" by pairing it with immaculate sailor pants, gold-tone buttons, and mules. The ruggedness of Brittany met the hedonism of the Côte d'Azur. Other functional garments such as the painter's smock, the peasant blouse, and the knit sweaters worn by Irish farmers and fishermen would be taken out of their original context and placed in forced "marriages."

His focus on uniforms would be further magnified when he added a unisex dimension to the paradox. In 1966, the Tuxedo, "Le Smoking," changed everything. For many years, the customary codes of eveningwear were low-cut evening gowns for women and tuxedos for men. During the nineteenth century, the satin-lapeled tuxedo was worn over a man's evening jacket to shield it from the ash and smell of cigars enjoyed in smoking rooms. But during the Roaring Twenties, it would replace the overly formal tailcoat. Saint Laurent "feminized" the first version of the Tuxedo, Number 76, by pairing it with an organdy blouse with a soft bow. From 1966 to 2002, the Tuxedo was featured—and expected— 230 times in the *maison*'s fashion shows. Open to endless variations, the Tuxedo had become a timeless icon.

Opposite page: First pea jacket worn by Heather, Spring-Summer 1962 haute couture collection. 30 bis, rue Spontini, Paris.

Yves Saint Laurent and Ulla
wearing a ready-to-wear
daytime ensemble in front of
the first SAINT LAURENT
rive gauche boutique,
21, rue de Tournon, Paris,
September 26, 1966.

First pantsuit, Spring-Summer
1967 haute couture collection.
L'Officiel, March, 1967.

The play between masculine and feminine continued as other garments typically associated with masculine virility and "bad boys" made their way into Saint Laurent's designs. The Winter 1967 collection pantsuit was inspired by film noir gangsters, the Winter 1963 motorcycle jacket by bikers, the trench coat by British World War I officers, and the jumpsuit by aviators. The exploration of unisex fashion culminated in the redesign of the safari jacket. Worn by Westerners during the nineteenth century in Africa and India, the safari jacket was meant to protect the wearer from the heat. Made of linen or cotton, its beige color blended with the desert sand. The jacket was a mainstay of both explorers and colonial armies and served as elegant camouflage wear for the gentry on safari. Lion hunters wore safari jackets, but so did the women who came to symbolize tropical glamour (such as Grace Kelly and Ava Gardner in *Mogambo* [1953], directed by John Ford). For his summer 1967 collection named *Bambara*, Saint Laurent paired intrepid explorers wearing safari jackets with examples of Malian artifacts. The iconic image of the safari jacket is immortalized in the famous photograph published in the August 1968 issue of *Vogue Paris* featuring Veruschka posing as a sensuous huntress in a safari jacket, armed with a gun and a dagger. The loosely tied jacket reveals both her naked skin and her proud femininity—she is sensual, fearless, and uninhibited. Created around the time of the May 1968 events, the safari jacket would redefine the concepts of masculine and feminine. In another emblematic photograph, Saint Laurent, Betty Catroux, and Loulou de La Falaise stand together at the opening of the London SAINT LAURENT *rive gauche* boutique in 1969; they have each adapted the safari jacket to suit their own look: wearing a safari tunic and thigh-high boots, Betty Catroux exemplifies rock and roll while Loulou de La Falaise plays the part of a well-bred young girl and Yves adopts an androgynous pose. Sexual roles were becoming indistinct and interchangeable, opening up the possibility of disturbing seductions. Men conceded part of their virility to women and women accepted men's feminine side. The safari jacket was one of Saint Laurent's essentials, a *type parfait*. As a stylistic paradox, it is both traditional and contemporary and epitomizes the couturier's credo: "For me, the avant-garde is classicism."[3]

Saint Laurent launched a ready-to-wear line for men in 1969. On November 10, 1971—a year marked by scandals—he opened a men's boutique on place Saint-Sulpice and hoped to replace the still popular hippie look with a new masculine elegance. His men's clothes, meant to reflect his own wardrobe, included a perfectly cut trench coat, beige velvet "artist" pants, a "feminized" black velvet blazer, shirts and ties in solid colors, and oxford shoes. Satin vests, flowered shirts, striped ties, tank tops with Greek motifs, and star-shaped rhinestone jewelry added a touch of glamour. Once again, gender and style distinctions were blurred in a mix of tradition and modernity, elegance and fantasy.

Betty Catroux, Yves Saint Laurent, and Loulou de La Falaise at the inauguration of the couturier's first London boutique, New Bond Street, London, September 10, 1969.

Opposite Page: Pantsuit, Spring-Summer 1976 haute couture collection. Jacket and pleated pants of pinkish-beige gabardine.

Jumpsuit worn by Anna, Spring-Summer 1975 haute couture collection. 5, avenue Marceau, Paris.

THE FINE LINE BETWEEN GOOD AND BAD TASTE

While Saint Laurent was revolutionizing the world of fashion and blurring the lines between different genres, there were still many areas that remained taboo. The concept of bad taste was one that haute couture—the guardian of the temple of "good taste"—avoided like the plague. Saint Laurent, on the other hand, harnessed its power as a creative tool, a source of new energy. "You have to break the codes of bad taste," he told *Le Nouvel Observateur*.[4] In his view, contemporary fashion could do with a touch of vulgarity. This idea was perfectly illustrated in his Summer 1971 collection, with its allusion to streetwalkers in leotards and fur wraps walking along the shady alleys of the Bois de Boulogne on a summer night. The models—some recruited specifically for the provocative show—were made up and coiffed with intentional tastelessness. But Saint Laurent, following his penchant for paradox, directed them to walk proudly, with the haughty demeanor of upper-class women. The effect was not lost. The clash between the symbols of bourgeois decorum and vulgar transgression would culminate in two films for which Saint Laurent designed the wardrobe: In *Belle de jour* (1967, directed by Luis Buñuel) Catherine Deneuve's ladylike clothes conceal her secret identity as a call girl, while Anny Duperey, posing as an elegant woman, appears completely uninvolved with her husband's dishonest dealings in *Stavisky* (1974, directed by Alain Resnais).

Saint Laurent would walk the tightrope between provocation and discretion throughout his career, playing a game of hide-and-seek with nudity. In the 1960s, his see-through blouses revealed naked breasts as feminists were burning their bras in a gesture of protest. Unlike the activists, Saint Laurent presented nudity in an ambiguous way, very "dressed," very "covered." The famous dress worn by Danielle Luquet de Saint Germain in the Winter 1968 show covered her entire body, with a jewel neckline and long sleeves. The dress was entirely transparent but a halo of ostrich feathers encircled her hips and the sheer chiffon fabric veiled her breasts. "When a woman loses her mystery, she is all finished forever. She has lost the most important thing she has," Saint Laurent explained to the Los Angeles Times.[5]

With his ability to operate on both sides of an issue and brilliantly manipulate the art of paradox, Saint Laurent established concepts that endure today. When designers and fashion critics speak of "mix and match," "breaking codes," and "irony" to describe the way a surprising contrast catches the eye, they are speaking about Yves Saint Laurent.

Opposite Page:
Coat, Fall-Winter 1966
SAINT LAURENT *rive gauche*
collection, worn by Catherine
Deneuve in Luis Buñuel's *Belle de jour* (1967). Black belted
slicker, sleeves of black
wool knitting.

Still from Luis Buñuel's
Belle de jour (1967) with
Catherine Deneuve.

Opposite Page: "Barbizon"
daytime ensemble worn
by Anny Duperey in Alain
Resnais's movie *Stavisky*
(1974). Coat of wool tweed
with black-and-white chevron
pattern, silver fox shawl
collar; belted tweed jacket; beige silk
satin blouse with bow collar;
black patent leather buckle
belt; flared skirt of black wool.

———

Original sketch for the
"Barbizon" daytime ensemble
worn by Anny Duperey in
Alain Resnais's movie *Stavisky*
(1974). Black felt-tip pen on
vellum paper.

Tuxedo with Bermuda shorts
worn by Danielle Luquet de
Saint Germain, Spring-Summer
1968 haute couture collection.

———

Opposite Page: Evening gown
worn by Danielle Luquet de
Saint Germain, Fall-Winter
1968 haute couture collection.

"I don't like too much fashion, I like clothes."

Yves Saint Laurent

The Alchemy of Style

The Symbiosis of Ornament and Structure

THE DEMAND FOR PERFECTION

Pierre Bergé once said that Saint Laurent was as "... French as André Le Nôtre; a man of precision in a world of imprecision."[1] Saint Laurent was a master of both shape and ornament. His style represented the perfect alchemy of form and color. The choice of fabric, the color, the cut, and the assembly were treated with equal importance. And yet Yves Saint Laurent did not have the tailoring skills of someone who started out in an atelier and worked his or her way up, as did Gabrielle "Coco" Chanel or Madeleine Vionnet. Saint Laurent was, above all, an artist with exceptional drawing skills. His studies at the École de la chambre syndicale de la couture, while soon interrupted, provided him with an understanding of the techniques specific to haute couture. And while working at Christian Dior, he learned how all-consuming the fashion business could be. What distinguishes one *maison de couture* from other, less important ones is the expectation that its employees will do more than simply yet expertly reproduce a complicated design. An haute couture atelier must execute every challenge the designer can imagine on paper. Each *maison* sets its own rules that reflect the couturier's personality. The challenges themselves often motivate the craftsmen. Constantly meeting the demand for perfection, the Saint Laurent ateliers would become among the best in the world. In 1969, during a televised interview with Monty Modlinger on the occasion of the opening of his London boutique, the couturier was asked why a simple pea jacket from SAINT LAURENT *rive gauche* was so expensive: "It's because of the cut," he shot back.[2] The cut, the quality of the fabric and the finishing, and the methods of production all had to meet the standards of perfection demanded of a garment bearing the Saint Laurent signature.

Previous Page: Long dresses, Spring-Summer 1974 SAINT LAURENT *rive gauche* collection. *British Vogue,* January 1974.

Opposite Page: Evening gown, Spring-Summer 1985 haute couture collection. Iridescent neptune blue chiffon cape; strapless dress of draped lichen green and moss green chiffon with left side slit.

Next Page:
Evening gown (detail).

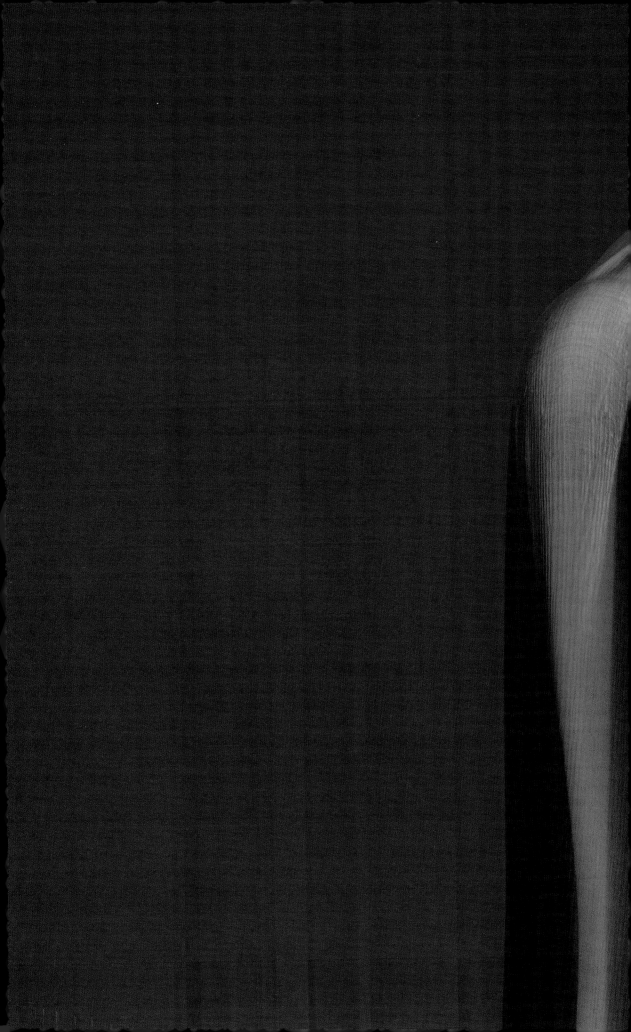

THE PREPARATION OF AN HAUTE COUTURE FINISHED GARMENT

The production of an haute couture garment was a complex process that began with an idea, a sketch, and a choice of fabric and resulted in a finished garment. Saint Laurent's drawings were precise and included specifics about ergonomics, the "drape" and the equilibrium that must be maintained between the fabric and the body. Executed by Yves Saint Laurent and then handed on to the *chef d'atelier*, the original sketch was the departure point for creating a design in the atelier. These sketches were done with a Staedtler 2B graphite pencil or, more spontaneously, with a felt-tip or ballpoint pen, on sheets of special drawing paper measuring 4⅞ x 12 ½ inches (12.4 x 32 cm). The same paper had been used in Christian Dior's studio. Yves Saint Laurent executed most of his sketches on these sheets until the late 1970s. A swatch of the fabric to be used for the design was often pinned to this sketch. The number of the atelier's specification sheet was also included, sometimes accompanied by notations.

Typically, the process would begin during a vacation in Marrakech, far from the excitement of Paris. It was there that Saint Laurent, in the Dar el-Hanch house, and later (as of 1974) in his Dar es Saada home, surrounded by the luxuriant Jardin Majorelle, conceived his collection. Once back in Paris, he would meet with his *chefs d'ateliers* and distribute his drawings. Sometimes these were assigned to specific people based on their particular expertise. The *chefs d'ateliers* then returned to their respective workrooms with the drawings and divided them up among the teams. Two or three drawings were given to each *première*, whose job it was to accurately translate the notations that appeared on the sketch onto a toile, the preliminary garment made of white cotton. The toile was then fitted on the *mannequin cabine* (fitting model). The presentation of the toile to Saint Laurent followed a protocol similar to a private fashion show. The workroom supervisor accompanied the model wearing the toile to a room where they would wait their turn before entering the second-floor studio overlooking the courtyard. The model would walk toward Saint Laurent, then turn around, in silence. The couturier examined the garment from every angle, whether directly or through the large mirror at the back of the studio. At times, he would use the silver-handled cane he inherited from Mr. Dior to point out certain details, and any required corrections were marked on the toile. The walls of the large, bright room with its thick white carpet were lined with binders, all manner of trim and accessories, and fabric swatches. The entire studio team, including Anne-Marie Muñoz and Loulou de La Falaise, would attend the fitting. Saint Laurent would sit at his modest desk—similar to a worktable—that was covered with statuettes of French bulldogs resembling his own dog, Moujik, and many 2B pencils and sketches. Though the fitting ritual was somewhat intimidating, the employees adored the "boss," for whom they had tremendous respect. Always courteous, Saint Laurent never failed to thank them or say a kind word. (When he ran into employees in the street, he always acknowledged them and even knew to which department they belonged).

Opposite Page: Yves Saint Laurent drawing in his home, Dar Es Saada, Marrakech, 1976.

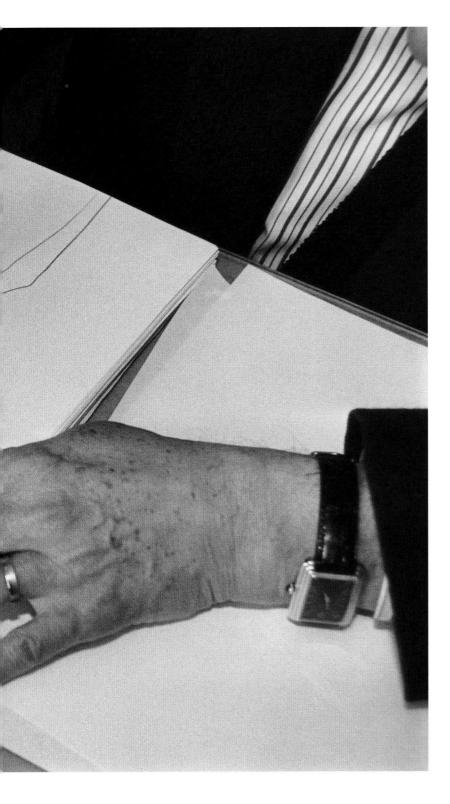

Yves Saint Laurent drawing
in his studio, 5, avenue
Marceau, Paris, 1991.
Le Figaro, July 11, 1991.

Next Page: Yves Saint Laurent
preparing his first collection,
11, rue Jean-Goujon, Paris,
December 1961.

Pages 102-103: Yves Saint
Laurent preparing a collection
in his studio with Loulou de
La Falaise and Anne-Marie
Muñoz, 5, avenue Marceau,
Paris, 1982.

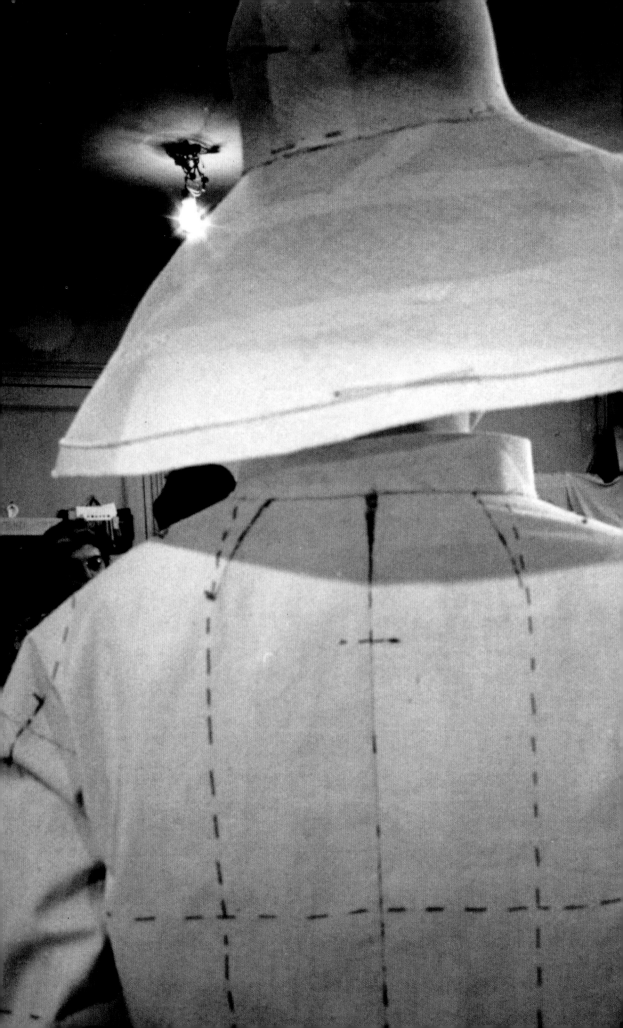

Jacket, Spring-Summer 1983
haute couture collection.
Black organza embroidered
with tortoise shell pattern,
embroidery made of nacre
and coral. Embroidery
by Lesage.

————

Opposite Page: Jacket (detail).

Yves Saint Laurent preparing
a collection in his studio, 5,
avenue Marceau, Paris, 1990.
From left to right: Monsieur
Jean-Pierre (head of the
tailoring workshop), a model,
Anne-Marie Muñoz (studio
director), and Loulou de
La Falaise. *Point de Vue*,
February 1998.

If, after three or four fittings, the toile was approved, it was ready to be translated into the chosen fabric. The toile was then taken apart and laid flat to create the pattern that would be used to cut the fabric. If the garment was to be embroidered, the motif was either drawn in pencil or a paper cutout of the motif was applied to the toile. Embroidery materials could then be ordered from the supplier. Fabrics were selected early on; delivered to the studio at the start of the collection season, rolls of fabric waited in a corner before being assigned to each specific garment. Occasionally, Saint Laurent assigned a fabric to a sketch before even having seen the toile. The selection of fabrics and embroidery was often based on a relationship of trust and understanding between the couturier and his suppliers. François Lesage made the embroidery for some of Saint Laurent's most celebrated designs, notably the Van Gogh jackets; the red sequined lips that were featured in the Summer 1971 collection were embroidered by Pierre Mesrine. Saint Laurent maintained a lasting friendship with textile manufacturer Gustav Zumsteg, the owner of Abraham, and Abraham's designer André Barrieu. The prints created over the years for Saint Laurent by the venerable and highly regarded Abraham fabric house became part of the *maison*'s identity—Saint Laurent's specifications were expertly translated into printed fabric. Each design was produced in several colors. Saint Laurent's most recognizable designs included geometric motifs inspired by Art Deco and Pop art, Picasso's harlequin patterns, tartan plaids, oriental designs featuring palmettes, leopard prints, and fabrics inspired by Greek ceramics from the fifth century BCE. Strong colors, boldly delineated motifs, *l'effet tableau*, and crisp graphics were emblematic of the Saint Laurent style. Before the fabric was actually printed, an "original print for patterned fabrics" was presented in the studio for revisions and approval.

When a finished garment was ready, it was "modeled" in the large Second Empire–style salon, where Saint Laurent would sit on one of the green damask sofas. Once the design was approved, Saint Laurent would choose among the many accessories displayed on trays. Any other embellishments were also selected at this time, including buttons made exclusively for the *maison* by many different craftsmen. Loulou de La Falaise was in charge of the fabulous jewelry: pieces crafted by Madame Denez, the trimmings specialist; strands of jewelry by Dominique Leroux; glass and lead pieces by Caillol; link chains by Ferrari. Hats were made in-house by a renowned haute couture milliner who could execute the master's vision: straw hats, conical Asian hats, men's hats, caps, soft toque hats. The milliners used a linden-wood mold sculpted by a hat-block maker or a "barded type"— a prototype made of wicker or cloth—to create the different hat shapes.

The process that first began as a sketch, then became a toile, and eventually an accessorized finished garment, could sometimes be simplified by skipping the sketch entirely. Saint Laurent might drape the fabric directly onto the model's body. He did this with increasing frequency until one day, Saint Laurent finally declared, "I can't make any decisions without them."[3] And by "them," he meant the models; in 1962, those models were Deborah, Paule, Morva, Heather, Françoise, and Fidelia, the first black haute couture model. Later, his models included Iman, Katoucha, Tatiana, Mounia, Rebecca, Cindy, Natasha, Amalia, Beverly, Diana, Eva, and Naomi. They were, he said, his "reality."

Opposite Page:
Yves Saint Laurent and Victoire Doutreleau during his first fashion show, January 29, 1962. 30 bis, rue Spontini, Paris.

Next Page:
Jewelry from haute couture collections.

THE REIGN OF THE "DRAPE" AND SIMPLICITY

During the early 1990s, the *maison* was comprised of thirteen ateliers and 194 employees who shared the *flou* (dressmaking) and *tailleur* (tailoring) responsibilities.

Saint Laurent insisted that his clothes be solidly constructed yet still remain soft and easy to wear. The use of interfacing, customary at Dior, was forbidden. Consequently, the ateliers had to combine the techniques of *flou* and *tailleur*. Working with fluid fabrics, such as Saint Laurent's cherished jersey, was indeed a challenge. Monsieur Jean-Pierre and Monsieur Jean-Marie were in charge of the main *tailleur* workrooms. Monsieur Jean-Pierre would eventually direct all the ateliers. The *flou* workrooms were the domain of Madame Felisa (later replaced by Madame Jacqueline), Madame Catherine, Mademoiselle Esther (who was eventually replaced by her sister Renée), and Madame Frédérique, who worked specifically on special orders for the theater. Madame Nicole ran the millinery atelier.

The workrooms that created the ready-to-wear prototypes were located in a building on Avenue George V. Its twenty-three employees were hired according to the traditional hierarchy of haute couture. At the top, the *chef d'atelier* ran the team based on his or her own set of rules. Directly under him or her, the *première main qualifiée* held the next most important position and could produce an entire garment under the supervision of the *chef d'atelier*. A *première main débutante* was not allowed to handle the "important pieces." He or she would begin with blouses and skirts. The *seconde main qualifiée* could finish a toile that had been approved by a *première*. The *deuxième main débutante* could finish a dress that the *première* had assembled, but only under supervision. Finally, the young apprentices were relegated to basting. It usually took a minimum of seven years to climb the ranks from apprentice to *première main qualifiée*. Each atelier had its own idiosyncrasies: Saint Laurent always wanted his seamstresses to be proficient in both *flou* and *tailleur*. When Saint Laurent hired Madame Felisa, formerly of Balenciaga, as a *flouteuse*, he was not aware that she had worked in the *tailleur* workroom. Felisa would become an exceptional *flouteuse*, whose mastery of the drape was legendary in the circles of Parisian couture. Madame Catherine combined the discipline of construction with the science of *flou*. "Almost" would not be tolerated; everything had to be "perfect." She warned her employees not to be tempted by the deceptive ease of *flou*. Saint Laurent detested darts so they had to be avoided as much as possible. The golden rule in all the ateliers was achieving the perfect drape. Madame Catherine's advice was to "let the fabric have its way—it's the boss." The other absolute was the notion of simplicity. A design should be straightforward and uncomplicated, even if the cut and seams concealed an elaborate and complex construction. The dress should be simple, straightforward, light, and easy to wear. Wearing a billowing black Saint Laurent ball gown, Loulou de La Falaise

Opposite Page: Evening ensemble, Fall-Winter 1991 haute couture collection. Long tunic of old-gold lamé cut short in the front; voluminous pants of black silk satin with ruching along the hem.

told *Women's Wear Daily*, "A dress like this is as comfortable as an old sweater," a statement that was not social bravado but the truth.[4] Saint Laurent's most astonishing gowns were light as a feather, easy to walk in, and never constricting.

At the end of this uncompromising journey, the collection begins to take shape. Like the script of a film, the collection board includes the title, the clothing category, the season and year, and from left to right, a series of miniature sketches by the couturier, featuring the name of the *chef d'atelier*, followed by the fabric sample, the number of the *fiche d'atelier* (specification sheet), the name of the model, and finally the number and place of the look in the lineup for the fashion show. The *fiches d'atelier*—records of all the technical details, including fabrics, colors, and accessories—are kept together in a book referred to as "the bible."

Accurately named, the bible is the binder that the couturier and his colleagues will turn to again and again. The *fiches de manutention* (supply forms) were also included in the bible to keep track of the names of vendors, the fabric cost, and yardage, as well as other supplies. These documents are essential for managing the orders of the *maison*'s clients. Ordering an haute couture garment also follows a ritual. At least three fittings with the *premières d'atelier* or the *premières mains qualifiées* are required. Staying as close as possible to the original design, a preliminary pattern is adjusted to the client's measurements. During the first fitting, the measurements are checked against those of the client's personal Stockman dress form. Made of wood and fabric, the Stockman is a virtual replica of the client's body. Measurements are recorded in a *livre d'essayages* (fittings book). Using dress forms allows the ateliers to move forward in the preparation of a garment in between fittings with the client.

PRECISION AND FANTASY

Ornamentation was a question of balance for Saint Laurent, who was as concerned with restraint as he was with creating something spectacular. All the designers in his personal pantheon had addressed similar issues: Chanel's concern for comfort and movement, Dior's love of glamor, Balenciaga's flawless cut, Vionnet's sense of drape, Schiaparelli's use of color. Over the years, Saint Laurent would achieve that synergy: "The further I go in my work, the closer I get to acquiring what I always dreamed of: mastering the *flou*, the softness that I lacked in my early days. It was difficult for me because I had been schooled by Dior and that was a school that believed in rigor. It was only much later that the *flou* came to me and I owe it all to a *première*, the top Balenciaga *première*, who came to work with me. She told me that a dress must always look like it is about to fall off. That a man's smallest gesture should cause the dress to fall away."[5]

Opposite Page Top:
Research sketch, Fall-Winter 1976 haute couture collection, known as the *Opera-Ballets Russes* collection. Felt-tip pen and pencil on vellum paper.

———

Opposite Page Middle:
Original sketch, *Cubist and Homage to Braque,* Spring-Summer 1988 haute couture collection. Graphite pencil and pastel on vellum paper.

———

Opposite Page Bottom:
Original sketch, Fall-Winter 1976 haute couture collection, known as the *Opera-Ballets Russes* collection. Felt-tip pen and pencil on vellum paper.

41052 jean Ma

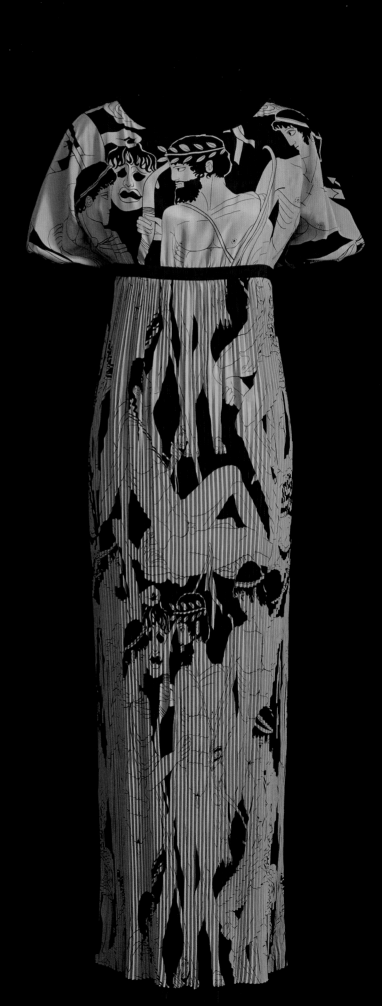

Opposite Page: Evening gown, Spring-Summer 1971 haute couture collection. Blue- and black-printed crepe de chine with pattern of ancient Greek figures; short-sleeved bodice with empire waist emphasized by black silk crepe bias tape; skirt with sunburst pleating.

Top: Atelier's specification sheet, Spring-Summer 1971 haute couture collection. Mixed media on thick perforated grid paper sewn with a fabric swatch.

Bottom: Supply form with names of the fabric suppliers Abraham, Carlier, and Billard, Spring-Summer 1971 haute couture collection. Mixed media on cardboard pinned with a fabric swatch.

SOIR

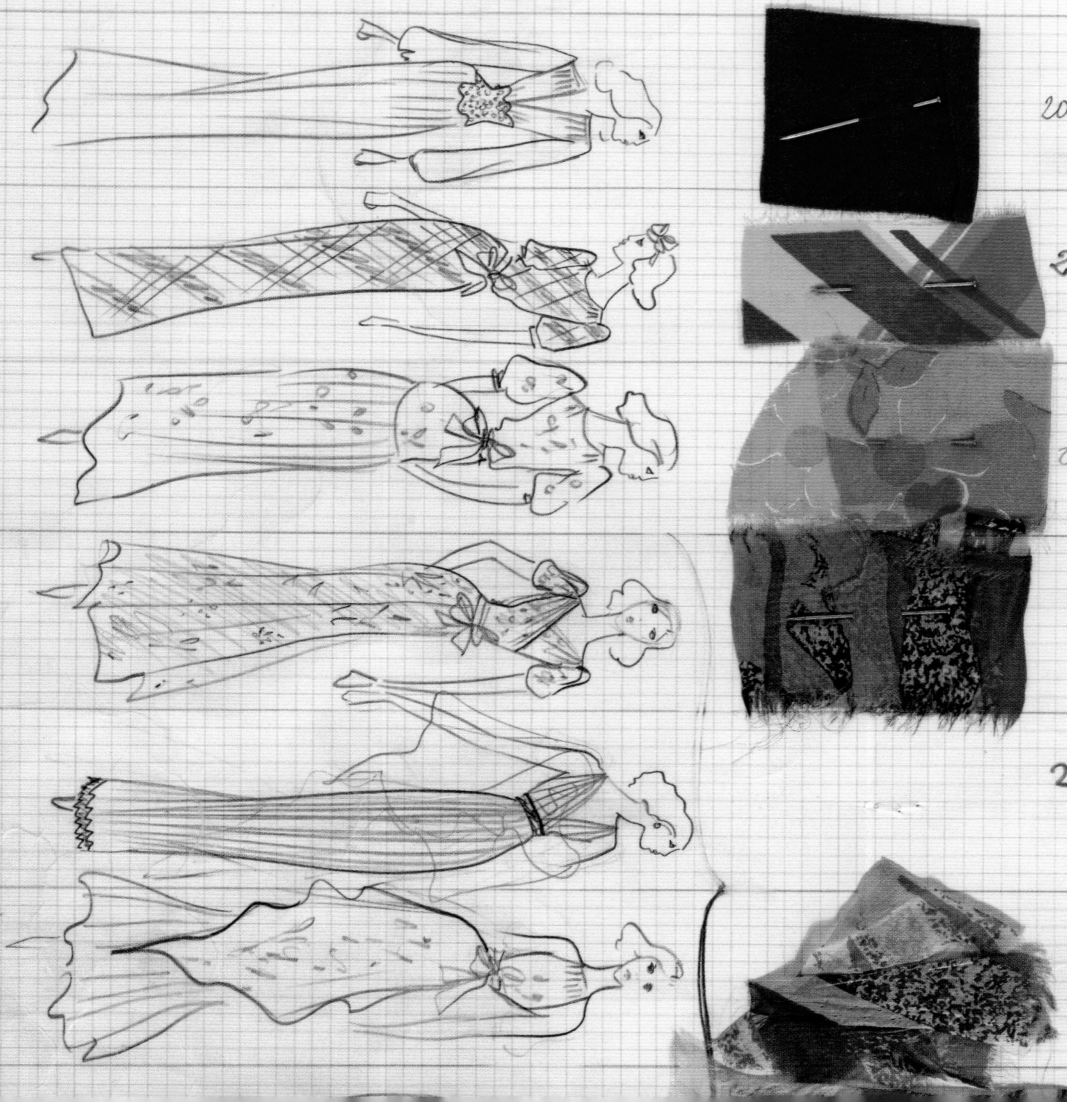

Esther	2067 / Annie	39 ✗
Esther	2069 / Barbara.	41 ✗
	2076 s/ Marie Thérèse	46 ✗
Blanche	2082 s/ Dominique	55 ✗
Catherine	2123 s/ Jacqueline	78 ✗
Blanche	2009 s/ Barbara	54 ✗

SOIR collection board, Spring-Summer 1971 haute couture collection. Mixed media on thick grid paper pinned with fabric swatches.

Evening ensemble (detail).

———

Opposite Page: Evening
ensemble, Fall-Winter 1968
haute couture collection.
Black suede sleeveless tunic
embroidered with jewels
composed of cabochons with
pink and green stones, fringed
trim; pink silk satin blouse;
black satin crepe pants.
Embroidery by Lesage.

Evening gown, Fall-Winter
1983 *Paris* haute couture
collection. Strapless gown:
draped pink silk satin bodice
with large bow on back waist;
black silk velvet skirt with
short train.

———

Opposite Page: Evening dress
worn by Gurmit, Fall-Winter
1990 haute couture collection.
Hotel InterContinental, Paris.

Yves Saint Laurent and one of
his designs for *Les Chants de
Maldoror,* a ballet by Roland
Petit, Théâtre de Chaillot,
Paris, 1962.

"I would have liked to be so many different things."

———

Yves Saint Laurent

Forty Years of Style

Nourished by Artistic Inspiration

ARTISTIC DREAMS

"I would have liked to be . . ." Yves Saint Laurent used that phrase repeatedly in his interviews, followed by a list of artistic and intellectual occupations, such as painter, set designer, director, writer, and more. Everything he would have liked to be belonged to the world of fantasy that would always inspire his oeuvre—the aesthetic universes of art, literature, theater, ballet, and film. "I would have liked to be a writer," he told Catherine Deneuve, adding, "At one time, I wrote a lot. And then I stopped because it was impossible to do both, to write and to move forward in this frightening profession that paralyzes me for most of the year. My mind is cluttered with dresses."[1]

He wrote his first poems at the age of twelve and his first drawings were book illustrations. In 1950, he assembled a curious collection of texts that he called *L'Amour,* accompanied by drawings in the style of Jean Cocteau. In 1951, in his own hand, he recopied the text of *Madame Bovary* by Gustave Flaubert, adding ink and gouache illustrations similar to those by Christian Bérard. Discovering Proust and *À la recherche du temps perdu* (*In Search of Lost Time,* or *Remembrance of Things Past*) marked a turning point in his life. Years later, when checking into a hotel, Saint Laurent would register under the name of Monsieur Swann, Proust's protagonist. His Normandy home, the Château Gabriel, was decorated in the Proustian style and the bedrooms were named after characters in *À la recherche.* In Proust, Saint Laurent recognized ". . . the one who was so interested in women and whose life was somewhat similar to mine."[2]

Along with the desire to write, he developed a passion for theater and film. In 1950 he discovered the magic of the stage after seeing Louis Jouvet's production of Molière's *L'école des femmes* (*The School for Wives*). In Oran, around the same time, he saw *Les enfants du paradis* (*Children of Paradise,* 1945), directed by Marcel Carné and starring Arletty—in 1966 he would design her wardrobe for Jean Cocteau's film *Les monstres sacrés* (*The Sacred Monsters*). Years later, he was the costume

Opposite Page: Evening gown, Fall-Winter 1966 haute couture collection. Straight dress of purple wool jersey, pink wool jersey appliqué.

designer for Edwige Feuillère when she appeared in *Cher menteur* (*Dear Liar*, 1982) and for Catherine Deneuve in *Belle de jour*, *La chamade* (*Heartbeat*, 1968), and *La sirène du Mississipi* (*Mississippi Mermaid*, 1969). His voyage of aesthetic discovery continued: Saint Laurent's aunt and uncle invited him to a performance of Puccini's *Tosca*. The sight of Maria Callas in a purple dress embroidered with black and fuchsia sequins struck him like a bolt of lightning. His obsession for Callas would last the rest of his life. He imagined himself as a set designer and tried his hand at making models. The sets and costumes he created in 1951 for *L'aigle à deux têtes* (*The Eagle with Two Heads*) and *Sodome et Gomorrhe* (*Sodom and Gomorrah*) showed astonishing maturity. Saint Laurent had already mastered the effect of theatrics and the power of costume. In 1978, his childhood dream came true when he designed the set and costumes for *L'aigle à deux têtes*, performed at the Athénée Théâtre Louis-Jouvet, which Pierre Bergé had just renovated in the Second Empire style.

After moving to Paris in 1955, Saint Laurent attended the theater regularly. He saw *Pour Lucrèce* (*Duel of Angels*) by Jean Giraudoux and discovered the productions of the Compagnie Renaud-Barrault and Cassandre. In 1956, he met choreographer Roland Petit and his wife, the dancer Zizi Jeanmaire. In 1959, Saint Laurent designed their ballet costumes for the production of Edmond Rostand's *Cyrano de Bergerac*. He would go on to design many costumes for Zizi Jeanmaire, notably the black leotards and ostrich feather boas that became her signature look. Rudolf Nureyev honored the couturier in 1981 by performing on the stage of the Opéra Comique before twelve hundred guests to celebrate the launch of Kouros, Saint Laurent's fragrance for men. Over the course of forty years, all of Saint Laurent's dreams—everything Saint Laurent would have liked to be—did, in fact, come true, either indirectly, through his diverse sources of inspiration, or directly, through his contributions to the theater, ballet, and film.

Opposite Page: "Homage to Zizi" embroidered sweater, Spring-Summer 1990 haute couture collection. Black organza sweater embroidered with black sequins and seed beads. Embroidery by Lesage.

ROMANTICISM AND MODERNITY

One of the most distinctive features of Saint Laurent's style is the tension between the dynamism of modernity and the melancholy of romanticism. Saint Laurent was drawn to romanticism's themes—the nostalgia of times past, the sweet sorrow of regret, an atmosphere of decadence, and the languor that defined the world of Proust. Great fantasies were triggered by visions of glory and decline: Visconti's *Il gattopardo* (*The Leopard*), the Tsar's court, the Forbidden City, the Spanish Enlightenment, the last maharajas, the Austro-Hungarian empire, Louis II of Bavaria. Themes of duality inspired the mix of opulent and modest materials Saint Laurent chose for his Boyar coats, Russian peasant skirts and blouses, Hussar jackets, tangzhuang suits, qipao dresses, Indian saris and sherwanis, black Bavarian corselets, or braid-trimmed Austrian jackets. Saint Laurent was fascinated by traditional costumes "... because these are timeless in terms of fashion. [...] And these clothes can be worn by women of any age. And that is one of my theories and one of my principles: that women of all ages can wear the same garment. That way, they all remain young."[3] The many "folkloric" inspirations that began with the theme of the maharajas in the first 1962 collection reached their apotheosis with the Russian, Spanish, and Chinese collections of the late 1970s.

TRAVELING THROUGH LITERATURE

Saint Laurent returned to the past and visited distant lands through his books: "... if I read a book about India, with photographs, or about Egypt where I have never been, my imagination can take me there. [...] When I saw Vermeer's *Girl with a Pearl Earring*, I could imagine what dress she might wear. And I think it is one of the most beautiful dresses I have ever created."[4] He bought all the latest art books from Galignani, the large bookstore on the rue de Rivoli. But it was the old masters and brilliant film directors, rather than images of folklore and travel, that first inspired Saint Laurent. From portraits by Diego Velázquez, Francisco Goya, or Thomas Gainsborough, Saint Laurent derived dark-toned dresses and little marquis outfits. A blue evening gown from the Winter 1981 collection brings to mind the soft crinolines and dazzling blue silks in Jean-Auguste-Dominique Ingres's 1845 portrait of Princess Albert de Broglie, the Countess d'Haussonville. Veils of chiffon that softly envelop the body are reminiscent of another painting by Ingres, *Odalisque with a Slave* (1839). Henri Matisse's use of intense colors and simple lines speaks to Saint Laurent's own restraint of line that he enhanced with a rich palette of colors. Saint Laurent's "Blouse roumaine" from the Winter 1981 collection was a direct reference to Henri Matisse's painting of the same name, which hangs in the Centre Pompidou. Another painting by Matisse, *The Large Blue Dress* (1937), in the Metropolitan Museum of Art, inspired a blue evening gown adorned with a white ruffle. Saint Laurent's taste for orientalism can be attributed to an even more direct source—his walks through the

Opposite Page: Evening ensemble, Spring-Summer 1977 haute couture collection. Romanian blouse of net chiffon and black lace; long loose-fitting skirt of coral faille with black silk velvet laps, trimmed with black passementerie.

Short evening ensemble worn
by Edia inspired by Henri
Matisse, Fall-Winter 1981
haute couture collection.
Hotel InterContinental, Paris.

———

Opposite Page: Short evening
ensemble worn by Danielle
Luquet de Saint Germain
inspired by Bambara art,
Spring-Summer 1967 haute
couture collection. Jardin
des Serres d'Auteuil, Bois de
Boulogne, Paris.

Opposite Page: Short evening
ensemble worn by Mounia.
Homage to Pablo Picasso.
Fall-Winter 1979 haute
couture collection. Hotel
InterContinental, Paris.

Short evening ensemble worn
by Sonia. Homage to Georges
Braque. Spring-Summer 1988
haute couture collection.
Hotel InterContinental, Paris.

souks of Marrakech, across its main square, Jemaa el-Fnaa, and in the Jardin Majorelle. "Majorelle is a Matisse painting; and it's my passion," he said about the property acquired in 1980 that he and Pierre Bergé would restore.[5] Saint Laurent's rather dark palette of colors began to change as of 1966. While he was in Morocco, he was drawn to brighter tones, contrasting shades, and warm colors. The djellabas, tunics and harem pants seen in the medinas were the inspiration for Saint Laurent's full-shaped designs, hooded ensembles, capes, and large draped coats. Orientalism was the bridge between the couturier's romantic soul and his attraction to modernity in the same way Sergei Diaghilev's Ballets Russes connected to Picasso. Saint Laurent's homage to Pablo Picasso, Georges Braque, Fernand Léger, to the Surrealists he discovered during his adolescence, Louis Aragon and Cocteau, and to the Bambara artists of Mali, have served as portals to modern art.

Piet Mondrian was the first modern painter Saint Laurent discovered, in 1965, in a book given to him by his mother. In Mondrian's paintings, Saint Laurent saw how the rhythm of color could be combined with a bold and forceful line. Before the huge success of the Mondrian dresses, the Dutch artist and founder of De Stijl was virtually unknown by the general public. But forever after, Saint Laurent would be considered an "... ambassador for culture, a visionary, guided by instinct and good taste."[6] The ideal meeting of color and construction remains a pillar of his style. To his detractors who underlined the ease or pedantry of artistic appropriation, Saint Laurent would quote Proust, who "... said that if one author admired another, he should not be afraid to imitate him, to find that which was so extraordinary, and take it further."[7] Regardless of the criticism, this artistic revitalization produced images that have enriched the public's imagination. There is no end of discussion in the media about how art invigorated fashion. *Observer Magazine* wrote, "It is this feast of visual pleasure that has kept Saint Laurent's name in every newspaper or magazine account of Paris fashion, as much as his sure line or powerful chic."[8] Still, the richness of Saint Laurent's inner life was not enough to explain his ability to create such astounding fashions. His talent was also evident in the manner in which he adapted his source material, in his way of transcending designs, blending periods and styles and adapting them to the present.

Meeting sculptors François-Xavier and Claude Lalanne was another important milestone for Saint Laurent. The partnership between the sculptor and the couturier was a unique experience for both Saint Laurent and Claude Lalanne; their fruitful collaboration would yield two iconic dresses, galvanized copper statues of women draped in chiffon by Saint Laurent, as well as jewelry designs that accompanied the couturier's creations. In addition, Saint Laurent commissioned François-Xavier and Claude Lalanne to create sculptural furniture for his apartment on rue de Babylone.

Another startling convergence of art and fashion took place on March 19, 1998, in London's National Gallery, when a dozen Saint Laurent models walked under the watchful gaze of Philippe de Champaigne's Cardinal Richelieu. The extraordinary fashion show celebrated the reopening—following a four-million-pound renovation—of the galleries housing French and Dutch paintings, financed in great part by a donation from Yves Saint Laurent and Pierre Bergé. Addressing the audience, the couturier said, "I have always believed that art is not only a part of culture but of life itself, that it should be made accessible to the greatest number and that museums deserve to be helped and encouraged."[9]

The final act of this artistic voyage—representing forty years of creation—would be the disassembling of the dazzling collection that Pierre Bergé and Yves Saint Laurent had acquired and displayed in their rue de Babylone apartment, followed by the sale of the Château Gabriel. In 2009, one year after the death of Saint Laurent, the public was invited to the Grand Palais to view the magnificently displayed private collection that included paintings by Pablo Picasso, Georges Braque, Piet Mondrian, Giorgio de Chirico, James Ensor, Henri Matisse, Le Douanier Rousseau, Édouard Vuillard, Edvard Munch, Juan Gris, and Giacomo Balla; sculptures by Henri Laurens, Constantin Brancusi, and Marcel Duchamp; and the drawings of Edgar Degas, Paul Gauguin, Édouard Manet, Paul Cézanne, Georges Seurat, Henri de Toulouse-Lautrec, Gustav Klimt, and Odilon Redon. The sale of the century marked the end of one of the most extraordinary artistic sagas of our time. Pierre Bergé had parted with all the art that had fueled the oeuvre of Yves Saint Laurent.

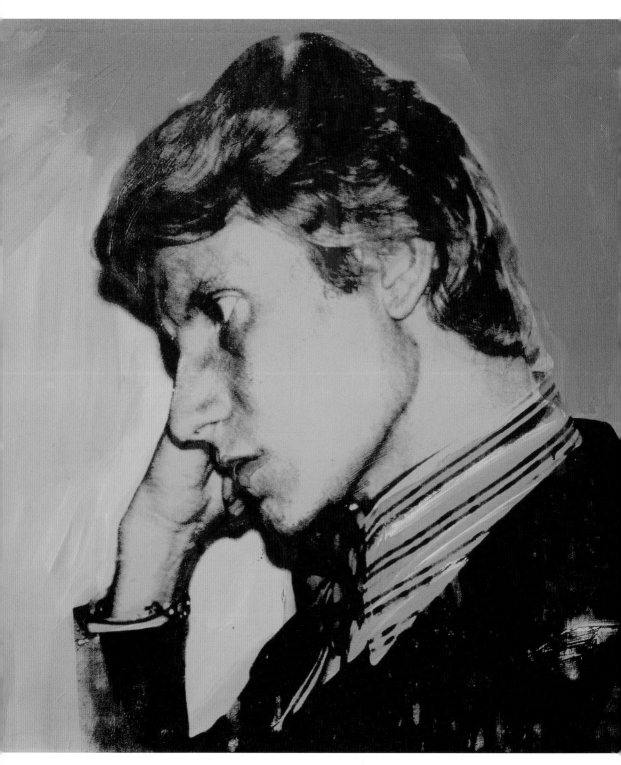

Andy Warhol (1928–1987),
portrait of Yves Saint Laurent,
1974. Silk screen on canvas,
39 9/16 x 39 9/16 in.
(100.5 x 100.5 cm). Fondation
Pierre Bergé – Yves Saint
Laurent, Paris.

"I am no longer concerned with sensation and innovation, but with the perfection of my style"

—

Yves Saint Laurent

Interview with Yves Saint Laurent

Over the course of thirty years, Yves Saint Laurent and Pierre Bergé have built an empire that brought the brilliance of French fashion to the world. Today, Saint Laurent talks to us about women, his anxiety, and haute couture.

LE FIGARO: After thirty years of fashion, are you aware that you have become a mythic figure of global proportion?

Yves SAINT LAURENT: No, I don't think of myself as a mythic figure and I am still surprised when people recognize me in the street. I did feel that way a long time ago, but since I've been battling depression, especially these last two years, I really don't feel it anymore. Perhaps I am a legend, one I've created through my work ever since that fateful day when Mr. Dior appointed me as his successor. From the moment I presented my first collection, the *Trapeze* line, I have lived in a constant state of anxiety.

When did you first realize that fashion was all about style and that you were going to create the Saint Laurent style?

Right away. My very first collection included a navy blue pea jacket and a white sweater. Leather jackets with mink sleeves. Everyday clothes. Raincoats. Pant suits. When I introduced the pantsuit for the working woman, it caused quite a stir in America. In New York's famous 21 Club, a woman wearing pants and a tunic was turned away. To be admitted to the dining room, she had to check her pants in the coatroom and wear just the tunic—leaving her, in essence, in a mini dress.

Why are pantsuits featured in every one of your collections?

Because extreme femininity and an androgynous appearance create a feeling of contrast and confusion. I introduced the Tuxedo in 1966, reissued it in 1981, and have kept it in my collections ever since—it's a timeless design. I have friends who still wear their ten-year-old Tuxedos.

Do you believe you have a sixth sense and know instinctively how women want to dress?

Yes, I do, I have an instinct for fashion. But not right now. I have many sketches but that's all. I know that inspiration will come, it always does. The work I do unconsciously is still churning. The fabrics are churning, as well as the colors, and everything is moving along unconsciously in my mind.

Were there times when your famous sixth sense did not work?

Yes, in 1964, the models just did not inspire me. Choosing the right models is very important to me. I drape the fabric around them and, suddenly, an idea explodes. I don't talk to them very much but I truly love them: and they are all in love with me.

You attribute your success with the public to the fact that you have always had a love affair with the street. Yet you rarely go out. How can this "relationship" exist?

I don't go out anymore. Perhaps I will again later on. I have been less in touch with the street scene since I've been having health problems. When I was younger, I was part of it. But the last two years have been so awful—all the detoxification treatments—that I have lost my connection with the scene.

We are headed toward more austere times. What should women expect from you? Glamorous or more practical clothes?

Both. For as long as it's possible, I will create practical clothes for ready-to-wear and glamorous clothes for haute couture. People speak about the "wonderful silence of health." I like to think about the wonderful silence of clothing— when the body and the garment become one, weightless. When a woman gets dressed and nothing pulls or catches. Ease is the essential element of elegance.

Can a woman without great means still be elegant?

Absolutely. To look beautiful, all she needs is a black sweater, a black skirt, and a man she loves on her arm. Black is essential.

In your opinion, who are the world's most elegant women? Those whose clothes perfectly match their personalities?

I don't know all my clients, but Catherine Deneuve is a perfect example. But to find another woman quite like her . . . perhaps Mrs. Thomas [Nan] Kempner in New York.

Whom do you dream of dressing?

You want names?

Lady Diana?

What are you trying to uncover?

You . . .

Faye Dunaway. Yes, I would like to dress Faye Dunaway.

So you prefer tall blonde women?

No. No woman is harder to dress than a Swedish woman. And no woman is easier to dress than a woman of color. So much so, that this season, I have intentionally used fewer black models than usual. They exude so much power, so much elegance; it's wonderful but really too easy. This time I am going to try to do without black models. This will be the winter of blondes.

Is it true that the one garment you would have liked to invent is blue jeans?

Yes, it's true. After jeans, what else is there? It was the perfect garment for its time. That harmony is very important.

Through your fashion you have taken us around the world—to Spain, Japan, China, India, Africa, and Russia. Have you also traveled around the world?

No, but I have visited those countries in my dreams. Just looking at a beautiful book on India allows me to draw as if I had been there. That's the role of imagination.

How has your career been affected by what you and Nietzsche call "aesthetic phantoms," the artists whose works have nourished your imagination?

Movies and theater have influenced me enormously. Jean Cocteau, for example, was truly an enchanter whom I knew during the last two years of his life. Cocteau was an incredible figure who personified exuberance and tenderness, a man who was open to the world, not turned in on himself like Marcel Proust—though to me, Proust will always be the master. Proust was the one who spoke the most about women and whose life reminded me a little of my own.

I was also very influenced by Matisse in my use of color. When I started out, I only believed in black and it took me a long time to get used to color. Today, I think I use color brilliantly. Picasso also influenced me tremendously.

One year, I was struggling with my collection. It was high drama—nothing was coming. One Sunday, I went to look at an exhibit on the Ballets Russes and I discovered the costume designs that Picasso had done for Serge Diaghilev's *Le Tricorne*. The next day, I took a piece of black velvet and a blue velvet skirt. I inserted alternating velvet panels into the blue skirt and everything flowed after that. I remember it so clearly.

Could you live without haute couture?

Yes, I think so. If I did not have haute couture, I would adapt everything I know about it to ready-to-wear because they are two different professions. I could incorporate haute couture into ready-to-wear. And that day is coming. Haute couture will last as long as it can, but within ten years, it will no longer exist. Times change and you need to adapt. But I would derive the same joy from luxury ready-to-wear as I do from haute couture. My creative input will be the same.

Besides the creative work, what else do you do? Do you go to the movies, do you read, do you watch television?

No, I don't go out anymore, but that's because of my medical treatment. Sometimes I go to the opera but I don't read any newspapers or listen to the radio and I never watch the news. But I could watch if I wanted to because my assistant has a television in his room and I can pop in and see what is going on. I must have spent years without reading a newspaper. I prefer to hear things from others. Seeing an image of a woman lying on the street in Beirut or of a baby crying overwhelms me.

And you know what Proust said: "Nothing can interest a creator besides his own work." Assuming that my work is my destiny, this attitude should be very understandable.

You never look at what your fellow designers are doing?
Never.

Why did you decide to stage a fashion show at the Fête de l'Humanité[1]?
I wanted people who view luxury as something inhuman, even grotesque, to have the opposite experience, to feel as if a great outside force brought them a moment of great happiness. It was not politically motivated; it was a gracious gesture and a way for the people at the *Fête de l'Humanité* to discover fashion. Seeing my clothes made them dream and appreciate fashion.

You didn't think you were taking a risk that day?
I was quite afraid beforehand but I was also very touched by the welcome I received.

Do you consider fashion to be art, given that fashion depends on change and art is lasting?
Fashion doesn't change though people will try to convince you otherwise. Like art, some designs are timeless—but only some.

When you showed dresses that revealed women's breasts, was it to make people talk about you?
I did it because that fashion reflected the times. I created the first see-through dress in 1968. When my designs revealed a woman's breasts like the *Winged Victory*, I was harshly criticized in America. Three years later, I did it again. For my last collection, I wanted to portray a nakedness that was strongly based on Goya. I created a dress of black, red, and pink voilette. But in order to have the photograph published in America—which can be fairly puritan—I was asked to cover the nipples.

Had you not been a couturier, what would you have been?
A set designer.

In February 1992, you will be celebrating thirty years of couture. What does that mean to you?
An enormous amount of work and a great deal of love.

Retrospectives of your work have been presented all over the world: Moscow, New York, Beijing, Tokyo. Which country's welcome touched you the most?
China. The exhibition, done at very little cost, had an air of the surreal. And the Chinese people, with their frenetic desire to copy every design on small pieces of paper, really touched me.

You have the reputation of being solitary. Do you have many friends? Do you see them often, at home or at their homes for dinner?
Outside of the collections, I choose to live in total isolation. The two depressions I suffered, one after the other, did me a great deal of harm. I was terribly unhappy and badly cared for. The first time was at the Labrousse hospital. And one year ago, I went through a second depression that was so serious I had to be treated for delirium tremens. I had to be hospitalized for three months in a psychiatric facility. It was horrible.

When you suffered this depression and were absent from your maison de couture, who did the collections in your place?
No one took my place, but Loulou de La Falaise and Anne-Marie Muñoz helped tremendously. It was very pretty, I saw the photographs.

Could the House of Saint Laurent exist for a long period without you at its helm?
Not if I am alive. I would not accept it. The people, the buyers would not accept it. They would refuse out of love. Saint Laurent can only exist with me . . . at least while I am still alive.

---

[1] Annual music festival organized by *L'Humanité*, a French Communist newspaper. Saint Laurent was invited to stage a fashion show as part of the program on September 8, 1988.

L'Actualité
Monday, July 15, 1991
Yves Saint Laurent: Thirty Years of Glory, Thirty Years of Angst
After sharing his journey with us last Thursday, the most secretive of living legends opens up to *Le Figaro*.
By Franz-Olivier Giesbert and Janie Samet

PARIS MATCH

N° 464 SAMEDI 1er MARS 1958 50 Fr.

Afrique du Nord 60 fr. — Maroc 65 fr. — G. B. 1 6 — Belg. 10 fr.
Suisse 0.90 — Canada 25 cents. — Esp. 12 peset. — Turquie 85 piast.

Nos envoyés spéciaux en Tunisie et en Algérie
LA FRONTIÈRE NÉVRALGIQUE

DIOR SANS DIOR
Pour sa première collection
Yves Saint-Laurent, 22 ans,
lance la ligne « trapèze ».
Victoire et Christine pré-
sentent ici deux modèles
inédits de printemps.
Photo Rizzo

Chez Dior. Yves Saint-Laurent dévoile sa première collection. De bas en haut : *Refrain*. robe-blouse soie noir et blanc ; *Café de Flore*. tailleur tweed de soie sable et noir ; *Jeudi*. robe bure bleu baby ; *Bruxelles*. robe shantung sable ; *Bonne Conduite*. robe-blouse natté gris ; *Colonies*. robe shetland azur ; *Virevolte*. tailleur laine et soie gris et noir ; *Zouzou*. tailleur flanelle grise ; *Cannes*. robe toile azur ; *Hippodrome*. robe mousseline beige à pois ; *Dame Tartine*. tailleur alpaga marine.

MODE : LE RIDEAU SE LÈVE

REPORTAGE ODETTE VALERI - WILLY RIZZO.   *VOIR PAGES SUIVANTES*

65

Opposite Page: Yves Saint Laurent and his models Victoire Doutreleau and Christine Tidmarsh. "Dior Without Dior," *Paris Match*, March 1, 1958.

———

Yves Saint Laurent and his models. "Fashion: The Curtain Rises," *Paris Match*, March 1, 1958.

Ruling Christian Dior's dress empire, is a modest but iron-willed 21-year old -Yves Saint Laurent

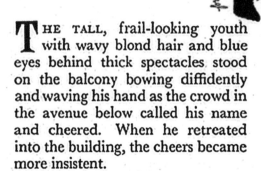

Crown prince of fashion

by RICHARD GEHMAN

THE TALL, frail-looking youth with wavy blond hair and blue eyes behind thick spectacles stood on the balcony bowing diffidently and waving his hand as the crowd in the avenue below called his name and cheered. When he retreated into the building, the cheers became more insistent.

"Go out again, Yves," a friend urged.

The young man shook his head. "No," he said, "it would not be proper. It is not me they are hailing —but the memory of the great Dior."

In that single modest statement lies the key to the character of a remarkable 21-year-old Frenchman, Yves Mathieu St. Laurent, who is expected to exert a profound influence on the dressing habits and style patterns of women all over the world for years to come. For Yves St. Laurent (his first name is pronounced "Eve") is the successor to Christian Dior, the designer whose New Look revolutionized dress design just after World War II.

When Dior died suddenly last year, St. Laurent went immediately into seclusion. Friends tried to get him on the telephone; he would not answer. For a time it was feared that he would never return to the House of Dior to work.

When he did, a week later, he was pale and seemed even thinner than

"Crown Prince of Fashion,"
Coronet, October 1958.
Illustration by Forde.

usual. "I am desolate," he confided to one of the *couturières*. "It is as though part of my life-stream were gone."

But when he was notified that he had been chosen to carry on in Dior's place, he appeared revitalized—as though he felt that he were giving new life to the man who had been his mentor. And his first collection, presented last January, caused almost as big a furor as did Dior's first. For the bony young man gave the world another new catchword, the "Trapeze" line.

Street demonstrations are familiar sights in France; but never before, until the Trapeze line appeared, had people gathered in the streets for the sole purpose of applauding a line of dresses.

St. Laurent seems slightly bewildered by all the attention he has attracted. He was pleased with the response to the Trapeze, which is a somewhat triangularly shaped dress line with a narrow top and a free-swinging skirt, but he dislikes publicity and fuss.

"Yves would have been much happier," one friend says, "if the House of Dior itself, and not he, had received the lion's share of the credit for his designs."

et Yet behind his modesty there lies considerable strength. "Yves knows exactly what he wants, and gets it," says Jean-Claude Donati, an executive at the House. And St. Laurent himself says, "I try at all times to do just what I wish to do. Before everything, I do what I please."

When a made-up dress is brought to him for the first time, he stands back, arms folded, and scrutinizes it carefully. If it does not please him, he has it destroyed, regardless of the cost of making up the model.

"I've seen him tear up patterns that other top designers would have given a year's salary to have produced," says one Dior official.

Yves is unconcerned with anything but getting the perfection he sees in his mind's eye. "I try to look at everything as though Dior were still looking over my shoulder," he says.

Dior was a hard taskmaster. When St. Laurent first showed him his sketches, the great designer threw out hundreds on the grounds that they were "too exaggerated."

"One must not push things too far," he said, "for that is one of the first secrets of elegance — genuine simplicity."

Later St. Laurent said, "I have never been impressed by anyone in my life but Dior."

He was so impressed, in fact, that he even adopted Dior's manners. Many French designers leap about, scream, beat seamstresses over the head with yardsticks, and generally behave like maniacs. Dior was exactly the opposite. He was gentle, courteous, considerate and retiring.

Also, he was concerned for the welfare of his workers. The rambling, labyrinthine series of five buildings at 30 Avenue Montaigne which makes up the House contain a hospital, a restaurant and recreation rooms for the employees.

St. Laurent is in the same tradition. He is a nervous young man, and seldom raises his voice. In fact, his speech is frequently inaudible. He answers most questions directly and with sensitivity. When he does not wish to commit himself, he will say politely, "I've never asked myself that question."

Nor will he argue. A designer recalls that, when his first collection was being prepared, one of the women in charge of accessories kept trying to push a certain alligator bag to go with the dress St. Laurent was inspecting.

"I don't think that one will do, Madame," he said.

"But Monsieur," the woman insisted, "it is absolutely perfect—it will be wonderful." And she went on at greater length.

"We will not use the bag, Madame," Yves said, mildly. And that was that.

It may be his calm disposition that enables him to work superhuman hours—he often goes without sleep for more than 48 hours at a stretch. He does not know where he gets his strength, his stamina or, for that matter, his talent. Neither of his parents were especially creative, he says.

St. LAURENT was born in Oran, Algeria, on August 1, 1936, son of a successful lawyer who was also in the insurance business.

Yves was the eldest child, and his mother's favorite (two younger sisters were born later and are now 12 and 15).

"I have a very strong relationship with my mother," he said recently. "She is very young, a good friend— but how can I explain what I mean when I am talking about someone I love. I am happy with her, that's all. And with my father, as well—

he is a gay man, very expansive, and exactly the opposite of me."

Their home life was secure. Yet he liked to withdraw to his own room and remain apart from everyone else for long periods.

"I read sometimes in my room," he says, "but because I had an absolute passion for the theater, I made a stage and created people. (He never showed his creations to anyone.) I have always wanted to remain closed within myself."

When he was 11, a production of *Les Ecoles des Femmes* arrived in Oran. Yves was taken to see it, and it changed his life.

"I was impassioned by the sets' elegance and simplicity, and the same with the costumes," he says.

He went back home and recreated the play in miniature. "I invented the costumes, taking little pieces of paper and bits and scraps of material . . . I did not know how to sew, so I cut them out with scissors and pasted them together. Let us not say that they were dolls. They were personalities made of cardboard which I designed and dressed and which I alone saw."

The family decided that Yves would study law, and he applied himself to it, he says, until he was 17. Then he told his parents that he wanted to go to Paris to test the talents in theatrical and fashion design he had been developing in secret. They agreed to let him.

Before leaving, he made sketches for a fashion collection—"simply to amuse myself." A friend in Oran gave him a note to Michel de Brunhoff, an executive with French *Vogue,* and he timidly took the sketches in for the expert to see.

Brunhoff was amazed. "I must take you to Dior at once," he said.

Christian Dior, at that time—it was 1953, in the fall—was just about the king of the fashion world. His 28 workrooms employed over 1,000 people; and the Dior empire embraced eight companies and 16 affiliated enterprises, spread over five continents.

From his earliest days Dior had taken a great interest in young people who wanted to learn the crafts of the fashion world. And, when Michel de Brunhoff brought in young St. Laurent, he readily agreed to look at the sketches. After an interview which lasted exactly 15 minutes, St. Laurent went to work as an apprentice at 30 Avenue Montaigne.

The master and the pupil had a strangely silent relationship. Each morning St. Laurent would go into Dior's spacious office, sit down, and silently watch the sketches being created. The two men almost never spoke.

"I learned more than I can ever say," says Laurent, "simply by observing. He seemed to have much confidence in me and I had some ideas that followed along with his. We worked without even discussing or talking. If I had an idea, I would design it, and show it to him—and he would nod, or shake his head, or sometimes point to details with a pencil, or perhaps redraw it on a fresh sheet of paper. Between us there was a silent power."

When Dior died, it was tacitly understood in the House of Dior that the master would have wanted no other successor than Yves. And so Marcel Boussac and his fellow directors met and elected him, placing the fate of a multimillion-dollar business on the shoulders of a 21-year-old.

St. Laurent's salary has never been published, but it has been estimated at approximately 630,000 francs per year (roughly $15,000). It is expected that, if his success continues, he will be elected a director next year or the year after that. Until then, however, he is still an employee.

St. Laurent has made few changes in the work routine that Dior established. The House presents four collections each year, and although each takes about three months to be prepared, one collection is often in the workrooms while another is being conceived in the minds of St. Laurent and his associate designers and fashion coordinators.

Before working on a collection, St. Laurent first produces nearly a thousand preliminary sketches. Then he and his four coordinators, all women, select the 200-odd designs that will ultimately be made into dresses. A collection usually requires 10,000 yards of fabrics and takes about 100,000 work-hours to complete.

Professional buyers from the smart stores order a limited number of copies of the originals, in two or three sizes. These dresses usually sell for between $400 for a street dress, to as high as $5,000 for an evening gown. Buyers from the mass-production houses lease the designs and sell the dresses, after an interval, for mass prices, sometimes as low as $6.95. Private customers who can afford the originals pay as high as $25,000 for a single model.

After the final showing, St. Laurent is in a state of utter exhaustion and goes home. He lives in a single room in a large apartment owned by an old lady on the Boulevard Pierre, and has lived there since he first went to Paris. He falls into bed and sleeps the clock around.

Yves leads a rather strenuous social life, appearing at most of the openings of new plays, at the ballet and the opera. More often than not he is in the company of Suzanne Luling, the sales directress of Dior. Although St. Laurent is a little over six feet in height, Mlle. Luling is even taller. They make a striking couple.

He is also seen frequently with Phillippine de Rothschild, daughter of a baron and a baroness. St. Laurent has said that he is in love with Phillippine, but does not know if they will get married.

"I don't think I could make a good marriage because I am so shut up within myself," he explains.

He believes that he has not changed essentially since he was a child, and those who have known him during his five years at Dior say his new authority has not altered his personality in any way.

"My biggest worry," he said not long ago, "is that I have had too much success too soon."

According to fashion authorities, however, the slender youngster from Algiers need have no worries on this score. His 1958 fall collection, "the curve line"—accenting high bodices and lowering hemlines to 15 inches from the floor—met with the same critical applause that greeted the Trapeze line. Says a French editor: "Yves will be around for a long, long time."

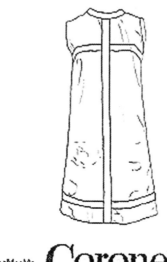

la folle nuit de saint-laurent chez régine

Le faste de l'or et de l'argent miroitant ou la douceur romantique du velours noir, deux contrastes pour le soir, deux styles de femmes chez Saint-Laurent; toutes les deux actuelles, toutes les deux nouvelles...

1. Argent. Une robe de dîner toute courte à petit col pointu, petites manches, à peine évasée. Raffinés, les boutons de strass. Broché argent d'Abraham. Bas argent brillant. 2. Or. Une autre robe de dîner toute simple, toute droite mais étincelante de plaques miroitantes brodées par Lanel. Bas or brillant. 3. Velours. Robe de gitane en velours noir à manches longues élargies et volants doubles bordés de tuyautés d'organdi blanc. Velours noir de Léonard. Chaussures Roger Vivier pour Yves Saint-Laurent. Coiffures Alexandre.

PHOTOS: LIONEL KAZAN PRISES AU « NEW JIMMY'S »

JACQUES CH

"Saint-Laurent's Crazy Night at Régine's," *Marie Claire* France, September 1966.

Next page: Evening gown and cocktail dresses inspired by Pop art and Tom Wesselmann, Fall-Winter 1966 haute couture collection. "Paris Fall Styles Full of Surprises," *Life*, September 2, 1966.

Paris Fall Styles Fu

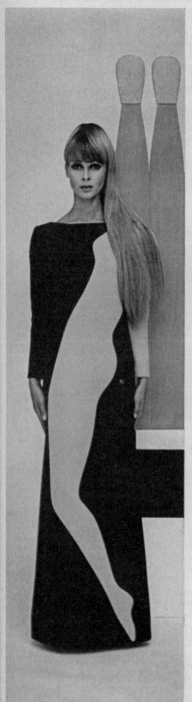

St. Laurent
rekindles youth's
pop art kick

In Paris this season, classic French elegance was supposed
big thing—until youth and internationalism asserted itsel
was Yves St. Laurent, for example, the young innovator
asserted his capacity to surprise with a zippy, varied and
stylish show that, among other things, Gallicized an Americ
age fad of some seasons back, pop art dresses. His motifs
not only such conventional ones as those shown above but
novations like the torso silhouette at far left and the big p

f Surprises

Made of jersey, a fabric that St. Laurent calls "the only mod-
material," the dresses are mostly short-skirted shifts. In clear
inspired by comic books, and worn with gold stockings and
e shoes, the outfits look just as incendiary as artist Raymond
's outsize book matches (from the current exhibit at the Iris
Gallerie in Paris) with which they have been photographed.
while the collections of other designers acknowledge the in-
tional give-and-take in equally stunning ways (*next pages*).

Photographed by JEAN-CLAUDE SAUER

PARIS
*Saint Laurent's
transparency,
bead-latticed midriff...
Bedouin stripes
for a red and white
beach cover by Grès*

Short evening dress worn by Twiggy inspired by Bambara art, Spring-Summer 1967 haute couture collection. "Paris the Way It Looks This Spring," *Vogue* U.S., March 15, 1967.

———

Opposite Page: Actress Charlotte Rampling wearing a pantsuit from the Spring-Summer 1974 haute couture collection. "New Allure in Paris," *Vogue* U.S., March 1, 1974.

IN PARIS

The new allure is: The woman comes first, and the whole feeling of dressing today comes through . . . the charm, the flirt . . . a little mystery. Everything turns on the ease and narrowness of the line . . . on the ultra-femininity of bias cuts in the softest of soft fabrics, the way they fit on a woman's body, and flow on the body, and move with the body. . . . The length of a skirt for day is just covering the knee . . . and the best-of-all day looks is still pants. No matter what the look—whether it's a perfect little tailored jacket, or an evening dress as ravishingly fragile as the most fragile lingerie—the seduction is there. It is Couture for a contemporary woman—an interesting, real-life, terrifically attractive woman. She's what every designer has in mind (and we had in mind when we asked British movie star Charlotte Rampling to pose for us on these pages). . . . We're not saying that there was nothing in all of Paris and Rome that we couldn't bear to live without. We didn't, for instance, choose a group of day coats in bright colors—the feeling now is for more basic coloring by day. We also decided against a series of glittery short evening dresses, even though we love seeing legs at night. But for the kind of evening where you'd wear that kind of short dress, there are newer, more alluring ways to be: the soft, beautiful evening blouse worn with pants—*the* pyjama of the year! . . . Saint Laurent's newest turn on his classic "smoking"—the most seductive small-evening look to come around the corner in years—and showing legs! It is modern, feminine, a joy to be in. It's a changing mood of fashion—to watch for. . . .

CHARLOTTE RAMPLING

109

LES BOUTIQUE
DE VOGUE

BRAVO A TOUS LES "SAINT LAURENT-RIVE GAU

◄ à Paris...
Marraine de la première "Rive Gauche" ina
21, rue de Tournon, **Catherine Deneuve** en

à Paris...
38, Fg-St-Honoré. **Betty Catroux** en cor

à Grenoble...
5, place St-Laurent. **Catherine Serre**, une

◄ à Madrid...
100, Calle Serrano. Devant le portrait d'Yves Saint Laurent, **marquise de Griñon** en redingote noire à boutons dorés.

à Munich...
Buerkleinstrasse 10. **Madame von Chamier** en tenue lamé.
▼

Les "Saint Laurent-Rive Gauche" font boule de neige. Aujourd'hui dix-neuf dans le monde. Demain, vingt de plus en Amérique. Au printemps, fleuriront Lausanne et Berlin. Adoptez, pour le meilleur prix possible, la plus jolie mode qui soit.

◄ à Bordeaux...
29, cours Clemenceau. **Madame Christian Laffontan** en robe longue de jersey blanc.

...gnona. La principessa ...calchi, ses achats termi-...es se ressemblent tou-...belle Hebey. Vitrines ...apis rouge orangé, siè-...ier Mourgue, lampions.
▶

à Nice...
7, rue Paradis. Sac en bandoulière et long pendentif doré, **Madame Jean-Pierre Vic**, jolie sœur d'Yves Saint Laurent.
▲

147

"The Boutiques in Vogue / 'Congratulations to All Saint Laurent-Rive Gauche' stores!," *Vogue Paris*, February 1, 1969.

LES BOUTIQUES
DE VOGUE *(Suite)*

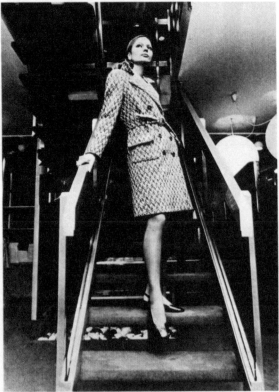

à Toulouse... ▲
1, place Wilson. Pardessus à chevrons pour **Madame Pierre Jonquères d'Oriola**.

à Genève... ▲
51, rue du Rhône. **Marina Doria** devant le choix des ceintures...

à Saint-Tropez... ▲
41, rue Gambetta. **La comtesse Charles de Rohan Chabot** avec l'écharpe à succès.

à Paris...
46, av. Victor-Hugo. Les pantalons larges **d'Albina**

elles...
e Waterloo. La robe-kilt à car-
ncesse **Antoinette de Mérode.**

ch...
La **princesse Theresa Fürs-**
le ciré dont tout Paris raffole.

à New York...
855, Madison Avenue. Un autre imperméable court, porté par **Madame Hilarios Theodoracopulos.**

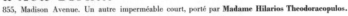

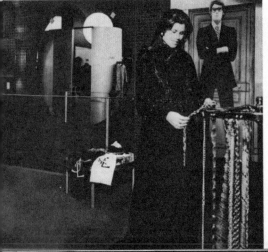

à Lyon... 10, rue des Archers (ci-dessus).
à Hambourg... Jungfernstieg 48.
à Venise... Hôtel Cipriani.

◄ *à Milan...*
18, via Santo Spirito. Tunique-pantalon scintillant et
ceintures-chaînes pour la **comtesse Dona Dalle Rose.** 149

"The Boutiques in Vogue /
'Congratulations to All Saint
Laurent-Rive Gauche' stores!,"
Vogue Paris, February 1, 1969.

Saint-Laurent façonne la robe autour des formes qui ont été modelées.

Cou, ventre, buste et les doigts sont sculptés...

... Comme ces fleurs devenues ici ceintures.

Claude Lalanne prend auparavant une empreinte sur le corps du mannequin.

Le couturier Yves S...

ent : les nus les plus habillés de la haute couture

r Claude Lalanne ont voulu qu'une ample mousseline contraste avec l'immobilité des formes moulées, et que les couleurs mettent en relief le cuivre doré.

Ce n'est plus le corps lui-même, mais le corps sculpté
que les robes d'Yves Saint-Laurent veulent mettre en valeur. S'il a divisé les spécialistes
en proposant pour cet hiver ses robes à mi-mollet, il a, en revanche,
fait l'unanimité avec ses robes du soir moulées. Saint-Laurent les façonne autour des objets
que Claude Lalanne a sculptés à partir d'empreintes du corps. Les clientes ne devront pas seulement faire
prendre leurs mesures pour la robe : elles devront aller à 100 kilomètres de Paris,
dans la petite ferme de Claude Lalanne, loin des quartiers traditionnels de la haute couture,
pour faire prendre l'empreinte de leur corps.

63

Evening gowns with waist and
bust sculptures in galvanized
copper by artist Claude
Lalanne worn by Dominique
and Lisa, Fall-Winter 1969
haute couture collection.
"Yves Saint Laurent: The Most
Fully Clothed Nudes of Haute
Couture," *Paris Match*,
August 23, 1969.

Yves Saint Laurent and Catherine Deneuve, both wearing tuxedos. "Yves Saint Laurent: 20 Years of Success," *Elle*, February 1, 1982.

Opposite Page: "The Last Emperor," *The Sunday Times Magazine*, October 9, 1994.

The Magazine

THE LAST EMPEROR

Yves Saint Laurent talks frankly to Edmund White

Notes

YSL: The Perfection of Style

1. *Yves Saint Laurent and Fashion Photography.* New York: teNeues Publishing Co., 1999, p. 176.

The Style of Now

1. Franck Maubert, "Yves Saint Laurent par Catherine Deneuve," *Globe* (1986), pp. 61, 56.

2. Hector Bianciotti, "La solitude et le plaisir," Arts et Spectacles, *Le Nouvel Observateur* (1986), p. 106.

3. *Yves Saint Laurent.* Paris: Éditions de la Martinière and Fondation Pierre Bergé – Yves Saint Laurent, 2010 and New York: Abrams, 2010, p. 38.

4. Catherine Guérard, "Portrait d'un jeune homme à la tête d'un empire," *Elle*, no. 623 (December 16, 1958).

5. "Sur le style 'Petite fille,'"*Elle,* no. 636 (March 3, 1958).

6. *Herald Tribune* (January 31, 1958).

7. Press release for the 1959 collection. Archives Fondation Pierre Bergé – Yves Saint Laurent.

8. Colombe Pringle, "Yves Saint Laurent sanctifié, il entre au musée," *Elle* (1986), p. 66.

9. Dino Buzzati, *Corriere della Serra* (January 30, 1962).

10. "The Rites of Fashion," *Newsweek* (August 12, 1963), p. 38.

11. Interview with Pierre Bergé, *FM* (October 15, 2009).

12. Barbara Schwarm, "Yves Saint Laurent: 30 ans déjà et la gaieté retrouvée," *L'Officiel* (December 1991– January 1992), p. 117.

13. "People: Yves Saint Laurent Finds a Gimmick," *International Herald Tribune* (November 6, 1971).

14. "Le 'côté biblique' du nu d'Yves Saint Laurent," *France soir* (November 12, 1971).

15. Interview with Colombe Pringle, *Elle* (1986), p. 65.

16. *Women's Wear Daily* (September 18, 1978).

17. Quoted in George Wayne, "Out to Launch," *Allure* (May 1993), p. 165.

18. Ibid., p. 164.

19. *Libération* (December 27, 1983), p. 10.

20. Ibid., p. 11.

21. Hélène de Turckheim, "Saint Laurent présente sa collection au Musée de l'Hermitage," *Figaro Madame* (December 13, 1986), p. 54.

22. *International Herald Tribune* (July 14, 1998).

23. Anna Wintour, letter to Yves Saint Laurent, Archives Fondation Pierre Bergé – Yves Saint Laurent.

A Liberated Style

1. Interview with Loulou de la Falaise, *FM* (October 9, 2009).

2. "Au fil des collections/Yves Saint Laurent," *Vogue Paris* (March 1971).

3. Sylvie Charier, "Quand Yves Saint Laurent parle," *20 Ans* (January 4, 1973).

4. Mariella Righini, "La France au parfum," *Le Nouvel Observateur* (August 16, 1971), p. 34.

5. Bettijane Levine, "The Mystery of YSL's 'Opium,'" *Los Angeles Times* (September 27, 1978).

The Alchemy of Style

1. Interview with Pierre Bergé, *FM* (October 9, 2009).

2. Barbara Criggs, "All about Yves," *Observer Magazine* (May 25, 1986), p. 38.

3. "Yves 92," *Vogue Paris* (1992), p. 187.

4. André Leon Talley, "Poufing along to Parties," *Women's Wear Daily* (July 11, 1979).

5. Franck Maubert, "Yves Saint Laurent par Catherine Deneuve," *Globe* (1986), p. 61.

Forty Years of Style

1. Franck Maubert, "Yves Saint Laurent par Catherine Deneuve," *Globe* (1986), p. 61.

2. Gonzague Saint Bris, "Yves Saint Laurent ou l'honneur de souffrir," *Femme France* (March 1992), p. 12.

3. Colombe Pringle,"Yves Saint Laurent sanctifié, il entre au musée," *Elle* (1986), p. 65.

4. Maubert, "Yves Saint Laurent par Catherine Deneuve," *Globe* (1986), p. 61.

5. Ibid., p. 54.

6. "Diana Vreeland expose un quart de siècle d'Y.S.L.," *Libération* (December 27, 1983), p. 10.

7. Hector Bianciotti, "La Solitude et le plaisir," Arts et Spectacles, *Le Nouvel Observateur* (1986), p. 107.

8. Barbara Criggs, "All about Yves," *Observer Magazine* (May 1986), p. 38.

9. Suzy Menkes, "A World of YSL and ART," *International Herald Tribune*, no. 35 (March 1998).

This catalogue was published for the exhibition *Yves Saint Laurent: The Perfection of Style*, organized by the Seattle Art Museum in partnership with the Fondation Pierre Bergé – Yves Saint Laurent, Paris, on view at the Seattle Art Museum from October 11, 2016 to January 8, 2017, and at the Virginia Museum of Fine Arts from May 7 to August 26, 2017.

FONDATION PIERRE BERGÉ YVES SAINT LAURENT

Special exhibitions at SAM are made possible by donors to ——————

SAM FUND FOR SPECIAL EXHIBITIONS

Presenting Sponsors ————————————————————

SEATTLE ART MUSEUM SUPPORTERS   **NORDSTROM**

Microsoft

Major Sponsor ————————————————————

△ DELTA

Additional Support
Contributors to the SAM Fund

Copyright © 2016 by Seattle Art Museum

Library of Congress Control Number: 2016935065

ISBN: 978-0-8478-4942-0 (Hardcover)
ISBN: 978-0-932216-73-1 (Paperback)

First published in the United States of America in 2016 by:

Skira Rizzoli Publications, Inc.
300 Park Avenue South
New York, NY 10010
www.rizzoliusa.com

In association with:
Seattle Art Museum
1300 First Avenue
Seattle, WA 98101
seattleartmuseum.org

For Skira Rizzoli:
Charles Miers, Publisher
Margaret Rennolds Chace, Associate Publisher
Caitlin Leffel, Editor
Alyn Evans, Production Manager
Florence Müller's text translated by Denise Jacobs

Design: Cristina Vásquez / Barboletta

2016 2017 2018 2019 / 10 9 8 7 6 5 4 3 2 1

Printed in China